Frederick Granger Williams = Annie Maria Jones
1836–62   1841–1901

Alexander Hale = Elizabeth Agnes Kendall
1838–1909   1845–1919

David Hyrum = Clara Charlotte Hartshorn
1844–1904   1851–1926

Don Carlos   stillborn son
1840–41   1842

Elber Aoriul
1871–1959

Frederick Alexander   Vida Elizabeth   Ina Inez   Emma Belle   Don Alvin   Eva Grace   Joseph George   Arthur Marion   Coral Cecile Rebecca
1862–1954   1865–1945   1866–1945   1869–1961   1871–1903   1874–1916   1877–1932   1880–1964   1882–1968

REFLECTIONS OF EMMA

REFLECTIONS OF EMMA
JOSEPH SMITH'S WIFE

Buddy Youngreen

Grandin Book Company
Orem, Utah

ISBN 0-910523-42-8

Contents

Foreword

Like the history of the Prophet Joseph Smith, the history of Emma, his wife, is entwined with the early years of the Restoration of the gospel. Emma has been known for good and for ill, and for many, she remains somewhat of an enigma. In recent years there has been a renewed interest in Emma Hale Smith. Several thoughtful studies of her life, at least segments of it, have been published. These efforts are part of a growing desire to understand and appreciate her, and to learn more about her family. Few are as well qualified as Buddy Youngreen to present a true picture of Emma.

Almost from the moment of his conversion to the Church, Buddy has had a "magnificent obsession" with the Smith family. His love of and devotion to the Joseph Smith, Sr., family has resulted in his travelling thousands of miles to become personally acquainted with hundreds of family members. President Harold B. Lee was wholly supportive of Buddy's desire to reunite the living descendants of the Smith family. In a Regional Representatives' seminar in April, 1972, President Lee spoke of Buddy's plans: "I had a young man come into my office the other day. He has become involved with the Smith family. He is trying to get the Hyrum Smith line, the Joseph Smith line, and the Samuel Smith line to come together in a kind of family reunion, hopefully that we might encourage some kind of better relationship." Now, because of Buddy's dedicated efforts the descendants of Joseph Smith, Sr., regularly meet in a family reunion. And because of his innate gift for instilling confidence and making friends Buddy has expertly bridged the gap in a divided family, and he has been the impetus that has encouraged estranged cousins to take first steps of reconciliation after years of bitter separation.

Foremost in Buddy's mind has been his intense interest in the lives of Joseph and Emma Smith; for many years he has studied and researched, and he has personally interviewed hundreds of their descendants. His keen desire to portray the love that existed between Emma and Joseph has prompted him to write and produce the play, *Yesterday and Forever*. Buddy has successfully shown that Emma was a very genuine person who contributed greatly to the Restoration and to the work of her husband.

During my sixteen years of acquaintance with Buddy, I have been impressed with his unusual ability to remember the names of living and dead members of the Smith family as well as a myriad of dates, places, and events. His diligence, competent research, meticulous documentation, personal acquaintance with hundreds of Smith descendants, and sensitivity to the diverse emotions and attitudes of the entire Smith family eminently qualify him to bring to us *Reflections of Emma*.

Eldred G. Smith, Patriarch
Great-great grandson of Hyrum Smith
27 June 1982
Salt Lake City, Utah

List of Illustrations

Preface

I care about Emma Hale Smith, Joseph Smith's wife. Because I care, I have searched back through the years in an attempt to learn more about her. My quest to understand her is based in my ongoing interest in Joseph Smith, which has grown to a continuous search for and examination of voluminous primary and secondary historical sources, coupled with a close association which I enjoy with hundreds of Smith descendants.

As in marriage the man is not without the woman, so is my study of Joseph Smith. I have felt it to be incomplete without an analysis of Emma.

The life of Emma Hale Smith Bidamon is a fascinating one. Emma's suffering from poverty and persecution, her pain at the premature deaths of her husband and many of her children, her devotion to her posterity, and her loneliness at the close of her life are all significant parts of this woman's history. Yet, all this would have little importance to the greater Mormon public were it not for her marriage to the Prophet Joseph Smith. Her relationship to him as wife, and mother of his children, and her role as witness and Elect Lady of Mormonism has inseparably connected her with the Restoration of the gospel. For these reasons alone, Emma's life is worthy of study.

Emma has remained too long on the outer edges of Mormon sympathy. Because she did not come West with the Pioneers, and because of certain statements made by Brigham Young and other early leaders, Emma has not been understood or respected. For example, it has been widely believed that Emma denied her witness of the Restoration, and that she repudiated her husband's divine call. Actually, there is little evidence to support such assumptions. Emphasis has often been given to Emma's and Joseph's marital problems, and Mormons generally have condemned Emma for supporting her son as president of the Reorganized Church. But to stress these issues without understanding Emma's motivations is unfair.

Emma had few interests other than her family. While the Prophet Joseph Smith lived she was immersed in the issues that confronted him. After the martyrdom, she was completely devoted to her posterity and her household.

Emma suffered greatly during her marriage to Joseph. What with frequent moves, constant persecution and poverty, numerous infant deaths, and lawsuits, she had little privacy and few comforts. While Joseph lived, she came to recognize that he belonged to the Church—she must share him and the family's resources.

This book points to what I believe are the most important and enduring themes of Emma's life: her sincere quest for religious experience, her possessive love for her husband, her compelling desire to bear children, her constant struggle against oppression, her deep commitment to her husband's divine mission, and her subjection to the ironies of her last years.

This volume gives attention to issues that continue to plague Latter-day Saints: Did Emma love Joseph Smith? Did Joseph love Emma? Did Emma, as a wife, support Joseph? Did she support him in his divine calling? Did she have a testimony of the Restoration? Why did she not go West? Why did she remarry? How did she die?

The first part of this book includes ten short essays depicting Emma's life in its various times and phases. The second part consists of interview notes taken by Emma's granddaughter, Audentia Smith Anderson. Audentia interviewed three of Emma's grandchildren who describe their memories of their grandmother. Copious footnotes and numerous photographs fill in background information.

In this book I have gleaned many precious reflections which I hope will increase understanding and respect for this elect lady.

I am grateful to H.G. "Bud" Fredrick, Jr., for his friendship and for kindly allowing me to publish Audentia Smith Anderson's notebook of interviews with Emma Hale Smith's grandchildren. Special appreciation is given to Richard L. Anderson, gifted scholar and long-time friend, for making the original typescript of the notebook. He has shared his exhaustive research of the Smith family with me, and his valuable insights into the life of Emma Hale Smith have influenced my thinking.

Thankfulness is also extended to Clinton F. Larson who, in September 1971, suggested a Joseph Smith, Sr., family reunion. I have often benefited from his ideas and editorial assistance.

Lyndon W. Cook, dedicated scholar and most patient of friends, has given unflagging encouragement to this project. He has read various drafts of the manuscript and offered many helpful suggestions in form and content.

I wish to thank Richard G. Ellsworth and Linda H. Adams who have contributed greatly to the style and readability of this book. Others who have helped significantly are Burnett B. Ferguson, Klis Hale Volkening, Clinton L. Oaks, Helen Schlie, Andrew F. Ehat, Sibyl Palmer, Gracia Denning, F. Michael Watson, and Patriarch Eldred G. and Hortense Smith.

I also respectfully acknowledge the warm expression of affection and help of Harold B. Lee, late President of The Church of Jesus Christ of Latter-day Saints. His undeviating encouragement and blessing have been a constant source of inspiration to me.

I have examined a vast amount of unpublished material at Church Archives, the Historical Department of The Church of Jesus Christ of Latter-day Saints, Salt Lake City, Utah; Library-Archives, the Reorganized Church of Jesus Christ of Latter Day Saints, Independence, Missouri; and Harold B. Lee Library, Brigham Young University, Provo, Utah. Thanks are given to the kind, talented staffs at these institutions. Also, I am particularly thankful to the owners and supervisors of many other widely scattered public and private collections that have been researched.

Finally, with affection, I am indebted to numerous descendants of Emma Hale and Joseph Smith. They have generously supplied me with copies of material in their possession in the form of letters, photographs, notebooks, diaries, and other memorabilia.

shed go to milk shed
milk pans for cats
– twice a day got full
kept farm clean – 3
shed & rats.
Catnip tea & they'd
lap it up.

Mend little Joseph's
coat for him deer
Knitty legs on list's
all this did & now
what think

Necessities in house
but no luxuries of
handsome furnishing.
Perhaps in go day had
settles – took pens of
Hotel of – 2 rooms
up stairs fitted very
beautifully – 4 poster
– closet built place
10 bedrooms too
small – bed wash
stand & chair

Editorial Comment

Audentia Smith Anderson's notebook of interviews with three grand-children of Emma and Joseph Smith is now in the possession of her grandson, H.G. "Bud" Fredrick, Jr., who has generously made it available to the editor. The interviews with Emma and Joseph's grandchildren—Emma Smith McCallum (eldest daughter of Joseph Smith, III), Frederick Alexander Smith (eldest son of Alexander Hale Smith), and Elbert A. Smith (only child of David Hyrum Smith)—were made while Audentia researched for her monumental volume, *Ancestry and Posterity of Joseph Smith and Emma Hale,* published in Independence, Missouri, by Herald Publishing House in 1929.

The photograph on the facing page shows the actual size of the notebook which contains thirty-three pages of penciled notes in Audentia's handwriting.

Every effort has been made to present a faithful copy of the notebook. Although many of the ideas are conceptually incomplete, a careful reading allows one to ascertain the intended meaning of the entries. A line-for-line transcription of the document is reproduced in this book. Spelling, grammar, and stylistic abbreviations have been retained with only minor punctuation added for clarity. Words placed within brackets have been supplied by the editor. The footnotes provide historical background and biographical information about individuals mentioned in the text.

PART I

BIOGRAPHICAL ESSAYS

Beginnings

Shortly after 5 o'clock on Sunday afternoon, the 28th of May, 1843, in "the Old Homestead" in Nauvoo, Illinois, Emma Hale Smith was sealed to Joseph Smith, Jr., as his wife for all eternity.

The ceremony was performed by Emma's brother-in-law, Hyrum Smith, the church patriarch. Hyrum understood as few others the love shared by Joseph and Emma; he comprehended the spiritual substance already woven into the fabric of over sixteen years of their civil marriage. Hyrum and Joseph were inseparable friends as well as brothers; with Emma, they were the presiding officers in the Church of Jesus Christ of Latter-day Saints. Joseph was president and prophet over the entire Church, Hyrum served as the associate president as well as the presiding patriarch, and Emma was the president of the Nauvoo Women's Relief Society.

The marriage sealing ceremony was part of a culmination. From the beginning of her life with Joseph Smith, Emma had struggled against oppression and separation, poverty and loneliness, and also fear and the agony over the deaths of her children. She had at last accepted these harsh realities, but not with abject resignation. Her faith in an unseen, divine power transcended the things of the world and gave her hope and strength. She was wonderfully and stubbornly devoted to Joseph, unfailingly intense in defending his divine mission. During the nearly eighteen years of her life with the Prophet Joseph Smith, Emma Hale Smith earned a place in the eternities next to him. The ceremony that Sunday afternoon in May, in which Emma was sealed to Joseph for all eternity, plus her reception with Joseph of the fulness of the priesthood, later that fall, attest to Joseph's grateful acknowledgment and recognition of that fact.

Nine months before, Joseph, in a few well-chosen words, had recorded his love for his Emma. She had just risked visiting him where he was hiding to avoid arrest on an island southwest of Nauvoo. Her courage and devotion and presence during this most desperate time profoundly impressed Joseph. He wrote of her, "My beloved Emma, the wife of my youth and the choice of my heart . . .here even in the seventh trouble—undaunted, firm and unwavering—unchangeable affectionate Emma!"

It is not known when Emma and Joseph first fell in love, but they first met at her home in Harmony, Pennsylvania, during the latter part of 1825. That year, Joseph spent a few months in the Great Bend of the Susquehanna working for Josiah Stowell. During this time, he boarded at the Hale household. By spring, Emma was being seriously courted.

Emma was a tall, attractive young woman with comely features. Dark-complexioned, with brown eyes and black hair, she possessed a singular, regal beauty of form and of character. She was intelligent, shy, and unworldly, having received strict Christian teachings but scant formal education. Emma was a year and a half older than Joseph, being twenty-one when she met him.

Joseph was six feet, two inches tall, fair-complexioned, and nearly twenty. He had penetrating blue eyes and light brown hair. Curiously, he combined a boyish shyness with a mannish self-confidence. His rough independence belied his awkwardness and lack of formal education and kept him from feeling inferior for lack of social experience. He would often say what was on his mind without regard for its appropriateness.

Joseph's meeting with Emma was providential. In time, Emma Hale would be designated the "Elect Lady" of Mormonism and Joseph Smith would be known as the "Mormon Prophet," but, during that bright spring and summer in 1826, they were just two young people falling in love. They were much like the nineteenth-century land in which they resided—undeveloped, vital and alive with a great spirit of promise.

Emma Hale was the seventh child of nine children born to Isaac Hale and Elizabeth Lewis. Born on the 10th of July, 1804, in Harmony, Susquehanna County, Pennsylvania, she grew to womanhood beside her mother and sisters becoming skilled in early American culinary arts, domesticity and the use of herbal medicines. She loved living by the beautiful Susquehanna River, and later, after Joseph's death, would not be able to bring herself to leave her Nauvoo home by the Mississippi.

Her uncle Nathaniel Lewis was a Methodist preacher, and Emma grew up in that faith. She was very devout, and the power of her spiritual promptings, even at a tender age, was often recognized by her family. Emma's father claimed that he was "converted from deism to faith in Christ" by Emma's humble prayer when she was seven or eight years of age. He had entered the woods by the house to hunt, and had come upon little Emma kneeling in prayer in his behalf. The sweetness of her simple prayer entered his heart and led him to faith in the Lord.

Joseph was the fifth child in a family of eleven children born to Joseph Smith, Sr., and Lucy Mack. He had grown up in New York State. Accustomed to hard physical labor, he learned early the virtue of work, toiling beside his father and brothers as he wrested a sparse living from the rocky New England soil. In those early years, Joseph considered himself a Christian, but he did not unite with any organized church. When others of his family attended church services, he stayed home and pondered the scriptures in solitude. He would often say, "I can take my Bible, and go into the woods, and learn more in two hours than you can learn at meeting in two years."

Sharing religious experiences undoubtedly drew Emma and Joseph closer together. To her ardent religious background, Joseph brought his own powerful witness of God's actuality and divine purpose. In quiet conversations with Joseph, Emma learned of sacred experiences which far transcended her own. It was not long before her wonder and awe at the tall young man so close to her turned to yearning and love. He was so powerful and strong, and tender and kind. Conviction grew in her as she listened to Joseph speak of angels and powers beyond this earth. And conviction and confirmation grew in Joseph as he discovered the deep faith and pure virtue that crowned Emma's sparkling beauty. That spring, in the brightening sunlight by the sleepy Susquehanna, Emma Hale and Joseph Smith fell deeply and everlastingly in love.

Isaac Hale took a rather jaundiced view of his daughter's new admirer. There was not much about the unlearned young prophet which impressed the austere Mr. Hale. After Joseph had finished his work in Harmony, he returned to call upon Emma. At last, Joseph asked Mr. Hale to consent to her marrying him. "This I refused," said Mr. Hale, "and gave my reasons for so doing." His reasons were simple. He found Joseph's elaborate religious experiences and low financial station very unfavorable. He sternly insisted that he would not under any circumstances countenance his daughter's marriage to Joseph Smith.

But love found a way, and for Emma and Joseph the way was elopement and a secret wedding. This was difficult for Emma, for notwithstanding her deep desire to marry Joseph, her parents' unwavering disapproval troubled her, and her strict Christian training made elopement seem closer to sin than to the will of God.

Later, Emma wrote that she had felt coerced into marriage. She claimed that she had had "no intention of marrying" when she left home to meet Joseph in South Bainbridge, New York. However, once there, she had been unable to resist the pressure of the intense young prophet. With guarded modesty, Emma declared: "Preferring to marry him to any other man I knew, I consented."

In stark contrast to the Hales' angry reaction to the marriage, Joseph's family gave their complete approval. Thus it was that Emma and Joseph went first to live with the Smiths in Manchester, New York, where they were heartily welcomed into an already crowded home.

The Sacred Record

Sometime during the early hours before the dawn of the 22nd of September, 1827, Emma went with Joseph from their Manchester residence to the Hill Cumorah, a few miles distant. They rode in a carriage borrowed from Joseph Knight, Sr., a Colesville farmer and friend. At the hill, Joseph obtained from the Angel Moroni the ancient record from which he later translated the Book of Mormon.

It is abundantly clear from Emma's correspondence that she knew that the Book of Mormon was of divine origin and that her husband was God's prophet. As the person closest to the Prophet, she was nearest the source and power of the Restoration. But there is little to indicate what her emotions were at this time. Surely she shared the excitement and anxiety of that early morning when Joseph left her with the carriage and climbed the hill to meet Moroni and receive the sacred record. Emma's father-in-law, Joseph Smith, Sr., recalled that moment in 1834 when he blessed Emma: "Thou shalt ever remember the great condescension of thy God in permitting thee to accompany my son when the angel delivered the record of the Nephites to his care." Indeed, Emma Smith was the first witness of the actuality of the Restoration.

She was not allowed to see the ancient record of gold, but she was perfectly "satisfied that it was the work of God." Joseph implicitly trusted

7

her; he knew that she would not violate the angel's command in order to satisfy her curiosity. Only certain chosen individuals commanded to bear public witness would be allowed to see the actual plates. Emma remembered that Joseph placed the plates on the table "without any attempt at concealment." The plates were "wrapped in a small linen table cloth which I had given him," Emma recalled. "I once felt the plates, as they thus lay on the table, tracing their outline and shape. They seemed to be pliable like thick paper and would rustle with a metallic sound when the edges were moved by the thumb." But she did not try to uncover the plates to look at them. When the Savior had been on earth, he had told the doubting Thomas that those who believed without seeing were more blessed. Emma believed and was blessed.

Throughout her first pregnancy, Emma was quite unwell; nevertheless, she helped Joseph as best she could. "When my husband was translating the Book of Mormon, I wrote a part of it," she recalled. "If I made any mistake in spelling, he would stop me and correct my spelling, although it was impossible for him to see how I was writing them down at the time. Even the word 'Sar[i]ah' he could not pronounce at first, but had to spell it, and I would pronounce it for him." She continued, "My belief is that the Book of Mormon is of divine authenticity—I have not the slightest doubt of it."

Unscrupulous people tried almost every means imaginable to obtain the golden plates for their monetary value. On one occasion, though sick and pregnant, Emma rode alone on horseback, with no saddle and with only a grass bridle, from Manchester to Macedon, a distance of several miles, to warn Joseph that an attempt would be made. Emma's willingness to undergo emotional stress and physical exhaustion attest to her commitment to her husband's divine calling.

In the hope of living a less harrowing existence, Emma and Joseph accepted an invitation to stay with her parents. Martin Harris gave the newlyweds fifty dollars to make the journey from Manchester to Harmony, Pennsylvania.

They arrived sometime in December, 1827, and about the time of their first wedding anniversary in January, 1828, Emma and Joseph moved into the first home of their own. Although the simple house was only a stone's throw from Emma's parents' home, being alone together in their own house had important meaning for the young couple. It symbolized, to them, freedom and independence. One story high, and only twenty-four by fourteen feet in area, the small house stood on the north bank of the Susquehanna River; it was to be their permanent residence for nearly three years.

Early in 1828, Emma was relieved of her secretarial duties when Martin Harris arrived from Palmyra, New York. He had great faith in the work and had offered to help finance the printing of the Book of Mormon. After helping Joseph complete one hundred and sixteen pages, Martin begged for permission to take the manuscript home to Palmyra to show his family. At length, permission was granted. But Martin Harris was not in control of his own household, and through a series of intrigues concocted by his wife, the priceless one hundred and sixteen pages of translation were lost.

Immediately after Martin's departure for New York, Emma gave birth to her first child, a son, Alvin, who lived only a few hours. Her sense of loss and sorrow are very nearly impossible to imagine; the death of her first-born weighed heavily on her soul. For several days she wavered between death and life, but at last she recovered. Bound together now by mutual love and suffering, Emma and Joseph accepted their heartbreak and loss. Emma knew from her own experience the reality of spiritual things, and the power of revelation from God to reveal answers to questions about life and death. Consequently, Joseph's vision in January of 1836, that "all children who die before they arrive to the years of accountability, are saved in the celestial Kingdom of heaven," brought her great solace and comfort.

As soon as Emma felt recovered from the childbirth and the loss of Alvin, she suggested that Joseph journey to Manchester to learn the cause of Martin Harris' long silence. Within a few days, Joseph returned with the tragic news that the manuscript had been lost.

How miserable now everything beautiful had suddenly become! Sweet hopes and close dreams had been thwarted with the loss of their baby, and the joy of success in the work of the Lord was now ended with the loss of all they had sacrificed so to achieve. The angel took the plates and the Urim and Thummim from Joseph, and he lost the power to translate. These were dark times. Everything and everyone, even the Lord, seemed turned against them. But the Lord was merciful, and Joseph was forgiven, and, in time, was once again allowed to continue the translation. Gradually, the sun began to shine again. There would be more babies. She knew that.

With Martin Harris gone, Emma again assumed her duties as scribe, but the translation progressed slowly. She and Joseph were in desperate circumstances. In order to have support from Emma's father, Isaac Hale, Joseph had promised that he would settle down and really try to farm, to try to make a normal living for himself and for Emma. But Joseph had no time to farm, and no interest; the demand on him to get the translation finished was more important than anything else. But he did try. And Emma tried, but she was constantly being torn between her parents and her husband. At last, providential help came in the form of food and money from a good friend Joseph Knight, Sr., and then, to their home one day, came Oliver Cowdery to write for Joseph, and things began to get a little better.

Pennsylvania to Ohio

Emma fulfilled her faith in the Restoration when she was baptized by Oliver Cowdery on the 28th of June, 1830, in Colesville, New York. Her baptism signaled her willingness to be cleansed of her sins by the restored authority. It had great significance for Joseph, for it meant that Emma, whom he loved with all of his heart, was willing to leave all the old ways behind and follow him.

Within weeks of her baptism, near the time of her twenty-sixth birthday, Joseph received a revelation from the Lord directed to Emma. She had been lately very depressed, and the loss of her baby, plus the constant poverty and persecution wore away at her heart. Emma was a woman of intense pride; she must have wondered many times whether she had not been meant for better things. But now the Lord told her that all would be well for her, that she would be blessed, that her sins were forgiven and that she was called to be "an elect lady." She was admonished to "beware of pride" and the things of this world, and not to murmur, but to trust in the Lord. She was told that her calling was to comfort Joseph with consoling words, in the "spirit of meekness," and to "go with him at the time of his going." She was promised that she would be a teacher among the Saints, and that the power of the Holy Ghost would be with her. And she was commissioned to make a selection of sacred hymns to be sung by the Saints

to bless their lives. The revelation was wonderful to Emma and en-
couraging; it filled so many of the empty places and strengthened her.

But now things were no longer right in Harmony. Persecution had
begun there also. Joseph had been arrested twice since June. Emma's
parents and family were embarrassed and angry. When the time came for
Joseph and Emma to go back to Fayette, New York, to meet with the Saints
in conference, confrontation with the Hales was unavoidable. Emma's
parents did not like her marriage; they wanted her to leave Joseph Smith.
Her father made it perfectly clear that if she went off again with Joseph
Smith, she would not be welcome ever again to return. She prayed and
wept and grieved "for the hardness of the hearts of her father's house" but
in the end she made the decision—she chose to go with her husband in
spite of all her family's tears and pleadings and angry protests and
prophecies. She was determined to stand by Joseph forever. Not that she
loved her parents less because she loved her husband more, but that her
commitment to him was more real to her than anything else on this earth.
But the decision was a terrible one— It meant a permanent separation from
her parents. She would never see them again in mortality.

Later that fall in Fayette, after the departure of Oliver Cowdery and
other missionaries to the western United States and the important
conversion of Sidney Rigdon in the Western Reserve, Emma and Joseph
decided to move to Kirtland, Ohio, where most of the Saints were then
concentrated. Early in February, 1831, when they arrived in Kirtland by
sleigh from western New York, it was cold and bitter, but Emma's heart
was singing for she was expecting a new baby and in Kirtland there would
finally be a house of their own and friends to be with, friends to trust and
love.

She and Joseph were very short of money. It was difficult. They lived
first with the Whitneys, and then with others, moving from place to place
so as not to impose too much upon others. It was embarrassing to be so
desperately dependent, but Emma was appreciative. She was in poor
health at this time, but she refused to favor herself. She was the wife and
companion of the Prophet, and like it or not, she had been called by the
Lord "an elect lady." Accordingly, she tried to set a proper example. Lucy
Mack Smith, Emma's mother-in-law, said, "I have never seen a woman in
my life who would endure every species of fatigue and hardship, from
month to month, and from year to year, [with such] unflinching courage,
zeal and patience."

As the time for her delivery neared, Emma could not forget the loss of
her first child. She was haunted by the fear that this child also would die.
Her worst fears were confirmed when, on the 30th of April, 1831, while

staying in a now-unknown home in Kirtland, Ohio, she was delivered of twins, Thadeus and Louisa, both of whom died within a few hours.

Emma was disconsolate. Years later, in a father's blessing to her, Joseph Smith, Sr., noted her heartache: "Thou has seen much sorrow because the Lord has taken from thee three of thy children: in this thou art not to be blamed for He knows thy pure desires to raise up a family." But for now, she felt empty. She wanted and needed living children, and she needed them now.

The next day, the first of May, 1831, in nearby Orange, Ohio, twins were born to newly baptized converts John and Julia Clapp Murdock. Within six hours of their birth, Sister Murdock died, leaving five motherless orphans. When Emma and Joseph learned of this, they asked Brother Murdock if they might adopt the twins and have them for their own. How wonderful it was and how thankful they were when Brother Murdock told them he was willing to do this. Soon the two babies, little Joseph and Julia Murdock, were taken into Emma's house and into her heart.

In the summer of 1831, Joseph left Emma and the new babies to the care of friends while he and others went to Missouri on a mission. Joseph knew the pain Emma always felt in his absence, and he tried to keep close to her by writing. It was a good practice which he continued throughout their married life. But for Emma, it was a trial of faith to remain at home alone without him, especially since Joseph received so much affection and admiration from the Saints wherever he went. Joseph was absent this time for only six weeks; by late August he had returned safely to Kirtland, and they were together again.

While waiting for the commodious rooms over Newel K. Whitney's Kirtland store to be finished, Emma and Joseph accepted a kind offer to stay with John and Elsa Johnson in Hiram, Ohio, some thirty-seven miles away from Kirtland.

Joint tenancy of a house was risky and difficult, especially as there were grown Johnson children still at home. Emma, Joseph, and the four-month-old twins occupied a room upstairs in the two-story Johnson home. It was crowded but would do, and Father and Mother Johnson were very thoughtful and kind.

However, shortly after Joseph and Emma arrived in Hiram, apostates began criticizing Joseph in the local newspaper, calling him names, and insisting that he was a fraud and a false prophet. Sidney Rigdon, who had also moved to Hiram, joined Joseph in publicly attempting to counter these vicious attacks, but the feeling in the town was bad. Some of the older Johnson children resented sharing their home with the Smiths. They often vented their feelings by tormenting Emma and Joseph. On the 24th of

March, 1832, a member of the Johnson family coordinated a night of terror for them.

The twins had contracted the measles, and Emma and Joseph had taken the sick babies into their own big bed in order to keep them warm. Near midnight, a mob burst into their room, and amidst Emma's frantic cries of "Murder! Murder!" pulled the warm covers from the bed and dragged Joseph out into the cold night where he was savagely clawed and beaten, poisoned, and tarred and feathered. Panic stricken, Emma screamed to the Johnsons to help, but there was little they could do but try to keep the sick babies warm and hope to be able to protect Emma should the mob return. In a short while, Joseph returned to the house alone; he was covered with blood and tar. When Emma saw him, she thought that the tar too was blood, and that Joseph was bleeding all over, and she screamed and fainted. Afterward, she and the Johnsons and other friends spent the remainder of the night removing the crusted tar from Joseph's scraped and bleeding body. In the days that followed, Joseph recovered, but little Joseph Murdock did not, he died from the shock of exposure to the cold night air and the ravages of measles. He was the fourth baby that Emma had seen taken from her.

Emma had little time to remain in uninterrupted mourning. Within a week after the mobbing, Joseph left on a three-month mission to Independence, Missouri. With infant Julia in her arms, Emma took little Joseph Murdock's body in a small coffin to Kirtland where she buried her adopted son next to her own little twins in the small cemetery north of where the house of the Lord would one day stand. Emma had thought she would be able to stay at the Whitney home, but she found that Sister Whitney, not knowing that Emma was coming, had taken in relatives to stay with her in her husband's absence; Emma had to look elsewhere for a place to stay. Reynolds Cahoon took her home to his wife and she stayed there for a few weeks, and then moved in with the family of Frederick G. Williams. The last month before Joseph returned, she stayed with Joseph's parents, Joseph Smith, Sr., and Lucy Mack Smith.

Kirtland Years

Joseph's return from Missouri was delayed at Greenville, Indiana, when Newel K. Whitney, jumping from a runaway wagon, fell and caught his leg, in the turning wheel, breaking his leg badly. Four weeks later than planned, Joseph arrived in Kirtland, and by late June, 1832, he and Emma and little Julia returned to Hiram, Ohio, to stay with the Johnsons. They remained there only a few months, for by September the upper level of the Whitney's store was ready for occupancy and for Joseph and Emma.

They were scarcely settled in their new home when Joseph had to leave again, this time to purchase supplies in New York City. Emma now was expecting her fourth child; no doubt she resented her husband's continual absences, necessary though they were. Joseph was keenly aware of Emma's loneliness and her fear of losing this child. He wrote to her from New York City on the 13th of October, 1832: "I feel as if I wanted to say something to you to comfort you in your peculiar trial and present affliction. I hope God will give you strength that you may not faint. I pray God to soften the hearts of those around you to be kind to you and take the burden of[f] your shoulders as much as posable and not afflict you. I feel for you for I know your state and that others do not but you must comfort yourself knowing that God is your friend in heaven and that you have one true and living friend on Earth your Husband."

Joseph returned to Kirtland on the 6th of November, 1832, thinking he had plenty of time before the baby should be born. But he was pleasantly surprised to find that the baby had been born a few hours before his arrival. What joy he and Emma felt at the safe arrival of a healthy son. They named him Joseph, III, after his father and his grandfather.

Emma and Joseph were constantly short of money and frequently found it necessary to borrow from Church members. But, at last, they now had a comfortable home of their own above the Whitney store. Now, Emma could create the domestic order she had so long been prevented from achieving. Here, at last, the Elect Lady might emerge as a woman of character. The pride she took in bringing order to her own home, and the contentment she possessed in having her own child opened her protective shell. She proved tender-hearted and generous to a fault; quietly, another side of Emma's nature, her courageous independence, began to find expression.

She loved her new home, and she liked it clean. One day she asked that Joseph's companions and followers cease their pipe-smoking and tobacco-chewing there. The school of the prophets was being held at her house, and she protested having constantly to clean up the mess the brethren left. Emma denied influencing or controlling her husband's mind. Modestly she declared: "Joseph knew that I wished for nothing but what was right [and] usually gave some heed to what I had to say." The Prophet's friends came to know that beyond her engaging personality and pious nature, Emma Smith had a will of steel.

Joseph inquired of the Lord concerning the use of tobacco, and on the 27th of February, 1833, the Lord revealed the "Word of Wisdom." Emma's strong desire to have a neat and clean home resulted in an inspired, far-reaching code of health, and Emma and Joseph were likewise able to settle a practical domestic problem.

After the construction of the Kirtland Temple commenced in June, 1833, Joseph was away from home much of the time. It was less painful now for Emma; she had a permanent place of her own and children to love and care for. Yet, Joseph's missions and business trips kept her actuely aware that she must share her husband with many others—Joseph was on the Lord's errand and could not selfishly isolate himself at home. In a sense, it was a measure of Emma's love for Joseph, a determination to make their marriage happy, that she never attempted to keep Joseph from preaching and travelling.

Joseph did try to be considerate of Emma's feelings and be a good father to the children. Her loneliness was somewhat compensated by his sensitivity, for there were many expressions of tenderness and affection.

Emma was only generally conversant with Joseph's business dealings, but she was very aware of what properties they owned and what investments were profitable. She suffered emotionally from the litigation in which he was continuously involved—so much of it was over their inability to repay borrowed money. Her awareness of Joseph's business concerns was an invaluable asset after his death in 1844.

In April, 1834, Joseph left Emma, Julia, and little Joseph, III, to make the exhausting forced march with Zion's Camp to western Missouri. Later that same summer, after his return, Joseph travelled to Michigan, preaching and teaching along the way. Usually, Joseph did not travel during the winter months, and on the 9th of December, 1834, family members of Joseph Smith, Sr., met for a special evening together. That night, Joseph, Sr., as the family patriarch, gave patriarchal blessings to many of his children, among them to his son, Joseph, and his daughter-in-law, Emma.

It was a tender blessing she received from her father-in-law whom she affectionately called "Father." Much of the blessing related to her relationship with her husband and children: "Thy soul has been afflicted because of the wickedness of men in seeking the destruction of thy companion, and thy whole soul has been drawn out in prayer for his deliverance." Regarding her desire to bear additional offspring, Joseph Smith, Sr., said: "If thou wilt believe ... thou shalt bring forth other children, to the joy and satisfaction of thy soul."

With the exception of a second short visit to the Saints in Michigan, Joseph did not make any long journeys from home in 1835. With Joseph at home, Emma's free time was taken in selecting hymns for Sabbath worship. Emma loved music; she had a beautiful soprano voice, but no formal training. The directive to compile a hymnal had been received in July, 1830, and when the hymnbook had not been forthcoming, lyrics suited to latter-day worship began to appear in *The Evening and the Morning Star*. Now, with time and with the talented help of William W. Phelps, Church printer and poet, Emma made every effort to complete the project. More than half of the ninety songs were borrowed from Protestant hymnals: none were authored by Emma herself. The little hymnal was at last printed by the end of 1835 and bound for distribution in February, 1836.

Emma's partriarchal blesing had promised her living children, and she gave birth to a second son on the 20th of June 1836, at Kirtland. Joseph and Emma named him Frederick Granger Williams Smith, after Joseph's close friend and counselor in the First Presidency. This time, Joseph was home for Emma's pregnancy and confinement.

However, within thirty days of little Freddy's birth, Emma again found herself alone with the children. Joseph had gone to Salem, Massachusetts, with his brother, Hyrum and Sidney Rigdon, and Oliver Cowdery. They were all so plagued with indebtedness. Joseph himself was personally responsible for some of the remaining costs for the Kirtland Temple. He and his colleagues hoped now to obtain some much-needed money to help pay these costs. But the journey failed in this purpose; however, many converts were made in Salem. On the 19th of August, 1836, Joseph penned a short note to Emma to inform her of his whereabouts and tell her of his concern for his family: "I thought a line from me . . . would be acceptable to you, even if it did not contain but little, that you may know that you and the children are much on my mind." The letter makes it clear that Emma should attend to their business interests: "I can think of many things concerning our business, but can only pray that you may have wisdom to manage the concerns that devolve on you, and I want you should believe me that I am your sincere friend and husband."

By 1836 or 1837, Emma and Joseph had moved from the upper floor of the Whitney's store to a house of their own. Yet, they enjoyed little privacy. With many of the Saints so poor, and housing in such short supply, it was not uncommon to find homes bulging with relatives and fellow converts. The membership of the Church was growing rapidly. Thousands drew spiritual strength from the Prophet Joseph Smith and his message of the Restoration. Streams of well-meaning, interested people called at the Smith residence day and night. There was little peace for Emma and less privacy for her family. Joseph was so unthinkingly hospitable to member and non-member alike that Emma was often obliged to share the family's food and beds to accommodate overnight visitors. Emma kept a good table for Joseph's guests, but thoughtless guests sometimes wounded her feelings.

Later, in Nauvoo, the many guests that crowded into Emma's house near dinnertime were officially informed by the Church newspaper to stay away because the Prophet's family could not be expected to feed the entire city. But even so, it was rare that Joseph ate at home without an invited friend. On one occasion, William W. Phelps suggested with a smile that the problem of so many uninvited dinner guests might be solved by having a smaller table. Emma quickly replied, "Mr. Smith is a bigger man than [that;] he can never eat without his friends."

Not only did others take advantage of Emma's hospitality and Joseph's time, but they often sought advantage in business dealings. Emma was annoyed when she discovered that some good Church members would unblushingly cheat the Prophet and his family out of their resources. These were hard times for everyone, and apostasy was rampant in Kirtland.

The year 1837 was particulary difficult for the Smiths. It was a depression year, and Joseph was gone much of the time, preaching and teaching, but also hiding to avoid false warrants for his arrest. Travel was costly no matter how necessary. Emma was left to manage all household matters. True to her trust, she competently dealt with the creditors and managed the business affairs. In May, 1837, Emma wrote to Joseph, explaining her frustrations: "The situation of your business is such as is very difficult for me to do anything of any consequence ... I have been so treated that I have come to the determination not to let any man or woman have anything whatever without being well assured that it goes to your advantage." She further declared that she was greatly irritated at Joseph's partners: "Everybody has so much better right to all that is called yours than I have."

After visiting Far West, Missouri, in November, 1837, Joseph decided to move his family there. But it would be difficult to leave Kirtland. Emma's attachment to Kirtland was both physical and emotional. Here she and Joseph had spent seven of their early years of marriage. Here, they had buried three of their seven children. Here, they had built a home and a temple to their God. Here would always be the memory of their first years as a family. Yet, it was at last with some relief that Emma and Joseph prepared to leave a city waning in spirituality and consumed by the fires of apostasy.

Missouri to Illinois

Emma feared anything that would undermine the stability of the world as she had inherited it. The decision to relocate in western Missouri was especially hard for her, but it had been made and she would abide by it. Knowing his life to be in danger, Joseph left Kirtland a few days before Emma and waited for her and the three children in Norton, Ohio, some sixty miles away.

Emma left Kirtland as she had arrived, carrying only her most precious things, her children and expecting now another child, travelling overland in the biting cold of winter, dependent upon the help of others, following her husband to a new place.

She left many memories behind, memories of service and love and kindness, and the glory of the beautiful temple—memories of loneliness, injured feelings, disappointed hopes and terror and abuse, and death, and three little infant graves. Westward lay the unknown. But she still had Joseph—she would follow him anywhere and be with him always.

The tedious journey by wagon across four states with three small children demanded patience and fortitude. The journey was wilderness. Rutted roads were frozen and bumpy. The rough ride aggravated Emma's nausea and made her back ache and her shoulders and chest. Joseph was kind and understanding, and there is no evidence that Emma complained, but it was a difficult journey. They arrived at last in Far West, Missouri, on the 14th of March, 1838. They came seeking serenity and safety, but the future there brought very little of either.

Less than three months after her arrival in the new Zion, Emma gave birth to her third living son, Alexander Hale. It was on the 2nd of June, 1838. Alexander's healthy birth was the only fond memory she was to have of Missouri.

Emma never knew a lasting contentment in her marriage or in her life. Demands on her for the Church's sake deprived her of the traditional values that Americans have come to expect: a permanent home, a secure job, privacy, respect, trust of neighbors, freedom of worship, and protection by the law. The most flagrant denial of all of these hopes and expectations was to occur in Missouri.

By August of 1838, a series of tragic confrontations had brought tension between Mormons and non-Mormons to a breaking point. Within weeks, Governor Lilburn W. Boggs, acting from misinformation and prejudice, issued his infamous order of extermination that Mormons must vacate Missouri, or the citizens of the state would be justified in taking their lives and property.

As prophet-leader of the Latter-day Saints, Joseph was singled out for harassment, persecution, and arrest. In November, 1838, he was taken from his home and falsely imprisoned for five and a half months in various Missouri jails, which ironically bore names such as "Independence," and "Liberty." Emma's stability was shaken. She found this latest arrest and imprisonment particularly long and painful. But there is no indication of self-pity, distrust, or recrimination. She was anxious to hear anything of her husband and of any progress toward gaining his freedom.

Once, in spite of the danger, she went with her brother-in-law, Don Carlos Smith, to visit her husband in jail. How she hated to leave Joseph "shut up in that lonesome prison." It was not right nor fair. He had done nothing wrong. And neither had she, or their little children. Why must they suffer so? Why couldn't they be allowed to live a normal life?

And Joseph. How must he feel? Falsely imprisoned, demeaned, starved, threatened daily with death, he could not help feeling deserted. What if Emma should lose her faith in him? "Oh Emma for God's sake do not forsake me nor the truth," he cried. In March, 1839, he asked: "Do you think that my being cast into prison by the mob renders me less worthy of your friendship?"

In her replies, Emma constantly assured Joseph that she stood strong beside him in his suffering: "The situation in which you are, the walls, the bars, and bolts, rolling rivers, running streams, rising hills, sinking vallies and spreading prairies that separate us and the cruel injustice that first cast you into prison and still holds you there, with many other considerations, places my feelings far beyond description . . .but I still live and am yet willing to suffer more if it is the will of kind Heaven, that I should for your sake."

The half year of terror and loneliness brought them closer together, but it was hard. It was the longest and most desperate trial she and Joseph had yet experienced.

Governor Boggs' extermination order forced the Saints to leave Far West. Again, in the dead of winter, Emma fled through tragedy. She and her children joined other Mormon exiles, moving sadly east, back towards the broad Mississippi. She crossed it on foot the 15th of February, 1839, picking her way carefully with the others across the rough ice of the frozen river. Under her dress, in tightly sewn cotton bags tied close to her body, Emma carried Joseph's private papers, including the valued manuscript of his inspired translation of the Bible. In her arms she carried her two smallest children, Alex and Freddy, while her two older children, Julia and Joseph, clung to her skirts. It was bitter cold, and she was more than weary, but in a way this was Emma's finest hour. Without her husband, she had done what needed to be done, and she had done it well.

She and the children were taken in by Judge John Cleveland and his wife Sarah. Their farm was about four miles from the village of Quincy, Illinois. Freddy was ill and Emma was again dependent upon the charity of friends. She had few ambitions for herself now, apart from her family, but it did seem cruelly unfair that she and the ones she loved should be shifted about so indiscriminately. Even so, she succeeded in keeping her wits about her, praying daily that Joseph would soon be released and be able to come home to her and the children.

Providentially, Joseph escaped from his false imprisonment on the 16th of April, 1839, and within the week was reunited with the Saints in Quincy with Emma and their four little ones. The separation, the longest yet experienced by the couple, had been an excruciating ordeal, but now they would build anew.

Emma and Joseph had a great need to be left alone, but this was an impossible dream. By early May, 1839, a new gathering place for the Saints had been designated some sixty miles north of Quincy. The place known then as Commerce, was soon renamed "Nauvoo" by Joseph. This Hebrew word meant "beautiful habitation for man" and connoted the idea of rest, something the Saints, in common with Emma and Joseph, had so much need of that spring.

Land was quickly obtained, and soon Emma and Joseph were settled in an old log structure affectionately known as the Old Homestead. Emma did not know it then, but Nauvoo was to be her permanent residence for the rest of her life.

During the summer, as the new city grew around them, Joseph's fatigue gave way to malarial fever, and it was left to Emma to nurse him back to health. Usually she could work steadily without seeming the worse for it, but this time she too became exhausted. Disregarding herself, she nursed Joseph back to health, and also many others who were sick around her, turning her house and yard into a kind of field hospital for the sick and dying. But there was little anyone could do, and malaria took a terrible toll of the Saints that year.

When Joseph was at last convalescent, he left Nauvoo to travel to Washington, D.C., to petition the general government for redress of the Saints' Missouri losses. The fact that Joseph had been so physically near while he had been sick made Emma feel even more keenly her loneliness in his absence. Little Frederick lay ill with the sickness, and Emma was again pregnant. Acutely aware of her condition, Joseph wrote from Springfield, Illinois, on the 9th of November, 1839, "Get all the rest you can," he encouraged, "I shall be filled with constant anxiety about you and the children until I hear from you and in a particular maner little Fredrick, it was so painful to leave him sick. I hope you will wach over those tender ofspring in a maner that is becoming a mother and a saint . . . .It will be a long and lonesome time during my absence from you."

Emma had Mother and Father Smith and her in-laws to befriend her, but for the needs of her soul she needed her husband; she must have looked each day for his return. For her, Joseph's long absences were forever frightening, and always resulted in surges of introspection and withdrawal. With death and the dying all around her, this separation would be no different.

Still, there was hope— On every side, an inspired people were miraculously building a new city in a day. It was plainly evident to Emma that these people had gathered to Nauvoo because of her husband, the Prophet Joseph. He was so courageous! And the Lord *was* with him. What an honor it was for her to be his wife. When she felt that the world was against her, she tried to remember that, and to remember that so many of Nauvoo's inhabitants respected her too, both for herself and because she was Joseph's wife. It was comfort to know she was loved.

In early 1840, Joseph wrote to her from Philadelphia to inform her that he was preparing to come home, and he prayed God to spare his family until he could see them once again. "I am now making all haste to arange my business to start for home. I feel very anxious to see you all once more in this world, the time seems long . . . . My dear Emma my heart is entwined around you and those little ones."

Joseph arrived in Nauvoo on the 4th of March, 1840. His trip to Washington was a failure, but he had learned much. He knew now that he must establish a city-state with plenary powers to protect his people.

On the 13th of June, 1840, Emma gave birth to her sixth son. They named him Don Carlos, in honor of Joseph's youngest brother. The birth was not difficult and the child was so dear, so round, and happy, and affectionate, but he lived only fourteen months, dying just one week after his namesake.

The death of a toddler is often more heartbreaking than that of a tiny infant. The long-lasting emotional intensity of Emma's distress at losing little Don Carlos is shown by a dream she had just before her death. She said that Joseph came to her and took her into a heavenly "mansion of light" where he showed her about from room to room. "One room was the nursery. In that nursery was a babe in the cradle. I knew my babe, my Don Carlos that was taken from me." She sprang forward, caught the child up in her arms and wept for joy. After a moment, she turned to her husband "Where are the rest of my children?" And Joseph replied, "Emma be patient, and you shall have all of your children." It was significant that she had seen little Don Carlos. Her other children had lived only a few hours. She had not come to know them.

Death came as no stranger to Emma and Joseph in Nauvoo. While they were living there, Emma's parents died in Pennsylvania, and death took members of each of Joseph's brothers' families, as well as his own beloved father. But even before little Don Carlos was laid to rest in the family cemetery near the Old Homestead, Emma was expecting another child. But the little boy was stillborn. Life was so unsure—any happiness Emma felt was fragile at best, and tragedy was not something one ever got used to. Regardless, Emma's faith in God did not waver. There is no evidence that she ever blamed the Lord for any of her misfortune.

I Now Turn the Key To You

Scarcely more than a month had elapsed after Emma's stillborn delivery when Joseph organized the Nauvoo Female Relief Society. On the 17th of March, 1842, in a large room over the Prophet's red brick store, Emma was chosen to preside over the society of the sister Saints. Joseph said that Emma's election to the presidency of the society was a literal fulfillment of her calling as "Elect Lady" in July, 1830. To Emma's previous ordination to "expound" the scriptures, was added now the authority to heal the sick, cast out devils, administer to the poor, and improve the morals of the community. Allied to the priesthood, the Relief Society did not have a written law; the voice of its presidency and the decision of its membership served as a "living constitution." Joseph taught "how the sisters would come in possession of the privileges, blessings, and gifts of the Priesthood," to hold "a portion of the Priesthood in connection with their husbands." The Prophet revealed that the Relief Society was worthy of significant autonomy and declared: "I now turn the key to you in the name of God and this Society shall rejoice and knowledge and intelligence shall flow down from this time." Because the sisters possessed "refined feelings and sensitiveness" and according to Joseph, "subject to an over much zeal," he cautioned them to achieve a careful balance between emotion and religious propriety.

Emma's calling in the Relief Society was her only official administrative responsibility in the Church, and the high-water mark of her Church career. She immediately applied herself to the task, gathering food, clothing, and furniture for the suffering poor of Nauvoo. Reports of her addresses to the regular meetings of the society show that she encouraged the sisters to be united in spirit and purpose and to purge out iniquity among the Saints.

Less than a month after the organization of the society, Servilla Durfee testifed that she had received a "great blessing" when Emma and her counselors anointed her with oil and laid on hands with prayer for the restoration of her health. She "never realized more benefit thro any administration [and] was healed, and thought the sisters had more faith than the brethren."

The years that Emma served as president of the Relief Society were difficult. Emma was appalled by the licentious conduct of John C. Bennett, and she took an active part in denouncing it. There was fear in Nauvoo that his "intrigues and false representations" might stir up animosity among the citizens of Hancock County, and result in antagonism and controversy. One thousand members of the Nauvoo Relief Society signed a petition addressed to Illinois Governor Thomas Carlin, praising Joseph Smith for his virtue, and requesting the governor to take action against Bennett. In July, 1842, in company with Eliza R. Snow and Lucy Mack Smith, Emma travelled to Quincy, Illinois, to deliver personally this petition and speak to the governor. Upon her return, on the 4th of August, 1842, Emma reported her visit with Carlin to the sisters, stating that she was unconvinced by his assurances of protection. Demonstrating her strong spiritual beliefs, she assured the sisters that they should "govern this generation in one way if not another—if not by the mighty arm of [government] power, we can do it by faith & prayers."

As if the Bennett scandal were not enough trouble for Emma and Joseph, the Prophet was arrested on the 8th of August, 1842, on charges of being an accessory in the attempted murder of Missouri's ex-Governor Lilburn W. Boggs. By luck, Joseph was temporarily released from this illegal arrest; he quickly went into hiding. The possibility that Governor Carlin of Illinois might approve of Missouri extradition proceedings so soon after Emma's interview with him was unthinkable to her. She was not awed by political position, but she had come to realize that in political position there was power. Accordingly, she decided to write her candid feelings to the governor. She penned two carefully worded letters to Governor Carlin in August, 1842, stating that Joseph was incapable of what was attributed to him. "My husband [has] not committed any crime whatever," she wrote Carlin. The charges against him were "the effect of unjust prejudice and misguided ambition, produced by misrepresentation and calumny." The whole affair was causing Emma "unutterable anguish." The conviction that breathes through these letters shows Emma's love and affection for Joseph, and her just indignation toward the evil actions of corrupt men in high office.

In support of her position, the entire society petitioned the govenor on the 5th of September, 1842, calling Bennett's published statements "barefaced, unblushing falsehood," and requesting the honorable executive to intervene in the extradition proceeding. However, all was to no avail.

During five months of hiding, Emma and Joseph maintained almost daily contact through letters and couriers. Secretly, Emma often visited Joseph in his hideouts, and when he could, Joseph made surprise calls at their home. The time was long for both of them. It put undue pressure on their marriage.

To avoid his enemies, Joseph thought of going to Wisconsin for six months, and he instructed Emma to make preparations. She replied by letter, hoping for other arrangements, but assuring him of her willingness to sacrifice: "I am ready to go with you if you are obliged to leave." Emma's love and support gave Joseph the courage he needed to endure.

Emma worried much, and perhaps to cover her concern, she worked harder than was prudent. In late September, 1842, she fell dangerously ill. She had not been in good health since her February delivery, and after Joseph's decision to keep out of sight, Emma's health seemed to deteriorate. Joseph tried to see her as often as possible. He feared at times that Emma might not recover. On the 5th of October, 1842, she was twice baptized in the Mississippi River for her health. She soon began to feel better.

Providentially, in January Joseph was discharged from the Missouri extradition proceedings, and he came back to Nauvoo, reassured and self-confident. There was great celebration and thanksgiving throughout the city the day he arrived. On their sixteenth wedding anniversary, Emma and Joseph hosted a grand party in the new Smith residence, the Mansion House, serving dinner to seventy-four guests.

Amidst all her fears and anxieties, Emma continued to work diligently in her calling as president of the Relief Society until the spring of 1843 when she learned for certain that Joseph was practicing plural marriage. Whatever her feelings had been before regarding the subject, she was devastated now by certain knowledge. In public, she continued as the official president of the society, but she functioned only at a distance. The weight of responsibility fell on her counselors, or on others. Extant minutes of Relief Society activities show that Emma attended no Relief Society meetings for ten months.

In early 1844, Emma, assured that Joseph had discontinued the practice of plural marriage, resumed with full vigor her work in the Relief Society. She "exhorted" the sisters to union and purity, and cautioned them to follow Joseph Smith's "public teachings" over any private ones, a subtle condemnation of plural marriage. Emma wanted to "see a reformation" among the Nauvoo Saints. On the 9th of March, 1844, Emma stated that it was "high time for Mothers to watch after their daughters & exhort them to keep the path of virtue." At the same time, she encouraged the publishing of an article in the *Nauvoo Neighbor* entitled, "The Voice of Innocence" aimed at condemning Orsimus F. Bostwick's vicious slander of Hyrum Smith and "certain females of Nauvoo."

Emma's leadership of the Relief Society ended abruptly as the society fell into disorganization during the tumultuous final months before and after the Prophet's death. But the creation of the society had marked the genesis of a new dispensation for Mormon women. The sisters had been given an institutional vehicle through which their unique contribution could be made and valued. Because the society had been formed according to a priesthood pattern, the women of the Church were able to function parallel to the brethren in the use of spiritual gifts—healing the sick, speaking in tongues, casting out devils, administering to the poor, officiating in temple ordinances, and looking after the welfare of the community.

Emma's presidency was foundational. Under her able but brief tenure as the society's leader, the divine purposes of religious service for Latter-day Saint women were identified. Emma's deep emotional involvement enriched the society and gave it definite meaning and relevance. The unmistakably spiritual tone and direction which Emma promoted, profoundly influenced the society's future.

The Ancient Principle

The concept of eternal marriage was privately introduced to a small group of friends by Joseph Smith in 1841. At the time, the concept of eternal marriage was inseparably connected with the doctrine of plurality of wives. Suddenly for Emma, the Old Testament practice, so familiar and benign, became menacing and alienating. The continuity with the ancient past that was so important to Joseph was not easy for Emma to accept; she was in constant alternation between acceptance of the doctrine and a scarcely masked fear that she might be condoning a great evil. Evidence of her fear and protest is voluminous. In moments of disbelief, she was plagued by a queston that she involuntarily asked herself: "In what way am I lacking that Joseph should need someone else?" Emma's struggle, both spiritual and physical, to accept these principles as revealed to her husband, constituted the greatest threat of her life, both to her love and respect for Joseph, and to her own sanity and self-respect.

As far as Joseph was concerned, living the ancient principle presented many unpleasant emotions, especially when he was forced to weigh his great love for Emma against his resolve to fulfill God's command. Had he not loved Emma so deeply, the introduction of plural marriage would not have been so difficult for him. Though Joseph was magnificently obsessed with his prophetic call, he nonetheless was a most sensitive husband and father, in many ways he was a model example. Delicately and carefully, he tried to teach Emma what he had come to know, that whatever God requires is right, no matter what men's traditions might be.

Emma's love and devotion to Joseph were obvious; yet she would have been scarcely less than angelic had she felt no jealousy. Almost daily, she vacillated between tenderness and anguish. Beset as she was by self-ridicule and worry, Emma, at times, became almost paranoid about being victimized. At one particularly unbelieving time, when questioned about the origin of the Old Testament practice, she responded with blind fury. Eudocia Baldwin Marsh asked, "Where did plural marriage come from?" With face flushed a fiery red, Emma snapped, "Straight from hell."

Apparently, there were times when Emma did logically accept plural marriage, but emotionally she never did. Joseph had begun teaching and practicing eternal-plural marriage in the spring of 1841, but neither Emma nor her brother-in-law, Hyrum, were aware of the Prophet's commitment and involvement until early 1843. Joseph, recognizing the potential dangers in the restored practice, deliberately swore all participating parties to secrecy.

Joseph was confident that Emma would finally understand and accept, and he delayed restoring the ancient endowment to women for at least a year. He needed and wanted Emma to help with that work. At last, in late May, 1843, Emma agreed. Joseph was overjoyed. Immediately she and Joseph were eternally married, and Emma received the temple endowment. She seemed at last to understand. Reconciled, at least partially, to the idea of Joseph's taking other wives, she swallowed her pride and announced to the prophet, "I will give you two wives if you will let me choose them." Accordingly, she chose Emily and Eliza Partridge and taught them herself the essential principles of plural marriage. Later she gave Sarah and Maria Lawrence also to the Prophet as plural wives. It was a notable sign of devotion to her husband.

Shortly after their eternal marriage, Joseph agreed to take Emma and the children to visit her sister's family in Lee County, Illinois. Emma needed a rest; she had been in poor health since the previous autumn. It would be a pleasant, uneventful trip, a chance for them all to relax, and an affirmation of affection between Emma and Joseph and Emma's people, and the sort of closeness with Joseph that Emma needed for the peace of her soul. But, unfortunately, the journey to Lee County almost ended in tragedy. Immediately after their arrival at Emma's sister's home, Joseph was violently taken into custody on the old Missouri charge of treason. He was brutally beaten and abused by the arresting officers and he and Emma were deeply embarrassed in front of Emma's family. At a time when Emma most needed the reassurance that mutual affection could give, Joseph was again taken from her, and she and the children were forced to return to Nauvoo alone.

After Joseph returned, freed from the extradition attempt, Emma began again to rebel against plural marriage. Even the written revelation failed to convince her that she should submit and obey. She took a journey alone to St. Louis in August 1843, and returned in a volatile mood. Angrily, she attempted to put a stop to Joseph's marriage practices by threatening divorce. In order to quiet her, and to gain time, Joseph said he would quit polygamy altogether.

But, even so, Emma was troubled. Maria Jane Johnson, a hired girl in the Mansion House, was a witness to these family problems. In the midst of the confrontation, Joseph sent Maria to fetch Hyrum. He was a natural mediator, especially between Emma and Joseph. Alone with her, Hyrum was at last able to calm her rage. "Brother Hyrum holds such a controlling power over my spirit," Emma said, "[that when] he comes to me and speaks to me I am melted to tears and I cannot talk back to him." The following day, Emma said to Maria Johnson, "You heard me finding fault with the principle. I want to say that the principle is right, it is from our Father in Heaven . . . but I am jealous hearted. Now never tell anybody that you heard me find fault with Joseph or that principle."

For all her hurt and fury, Emma truly loved Joseph, and fortunately for family peace, her threat of divorce came to nothing. Within three weeks after all the arguing, Emma had "turned quite friendly and kind" and Joseph made preparations for them to receive their highest blessings. On the 28th of September, 1843, Emma and Joseph together received the fulness of the priesthood.

Preludes to Parting

**E**arly in that tragic year of 1844, at the age of forty, Emma conceived a final time. She promised her husband that if the child should be a son, she would name him David Hyrum in honor of Joseph's brother.

Although Emma had been led to believe that her husband had discontinued his involvement in Nauvoo polygamy in August 1843, she yet warned a number of sisters to carefully watch their own husbands. On the 23rd of December, 1843, as she supervised female washings and anointings, Emma encouraged each sister to put her "foot down and keep it there," lest their husbands "take more wives."

During the early months of 1844, Emma and Joseph went often together to see their farm and visit friends. That April, two weeks after Joseph's famous King Follett sermon, Emma also traveled to St. Louis to purchase supplies for the Mansion House.

By May, Emma was in her third month of pregnancy; she was too ill to continue her regular household duties and had to remain in bed most of the time. Joseph cancelled many engagements to be with her. He seemed aware of his aproaching death and sought to improve their time together.

As May drew to a close, Joseph's enemies declared him a fallen prophet. William Law publicly made a number of libelous remarks about Joseph's private life, charging him in the circuit court with adultery, embarrassing

Joseph and Emma with the public charge of sexual crimes. Emma was filled with forebodings. Even the deep tenderness Emma felt from Joseph's daily presence was not enough to still her anxieties.

Two grand jury indictments, dated the 25th of May, 1844, were deferred until the next term of the court, but within two weeks Joseph was charged with riot in the destruction of the newspaper, the *Nauvoo Expositor*. Joseph thought of going to Washington, D.C., or to the West, in order to escape his persecutors, but he decided not to go. Instead, he resolved to have the charges investigated in Carthage. Emma was desperate. "I felt the worst I ever felt in my life," she said. "From that time I looked for him to be killed."

Joseph's death was almost inevitable. Political schemes from without and blood-thirsty dissenters from within forced his martyrdom. Though many were shocked when Joseph was killed, few were surprised. Sometime before midnight on the 27th of June, 1844, word reached Emma that her husband was dead.

Two white horses pulled the wagon bearing Joseph's mutilated body through the hushed streets of Nauvoo. It was unbelievable. The prophet of the Restoration was dead. The one solid anchor in Emma's storm-tossed life was gone.

The bodies were prepared for burial. Emma was overcome with grief. She fainted several times as she approached the bed where Joseph's body lay. Finally, she walked alone to him. Kneeling, she clasped him around the face and embraced his body. "Joseph, Joseph," she mourned, "have they taken you from me at last?" Thinking to comfort her, someone said, "This affliction would be to her a crown." Looking up with tears streaming down her cheeks, Emma replied, "My husband was my crown."

Thousands came to see their beloved prophet interred, but few knew that his body had already been secretly buried in the basement of the unfinished Nauvoo House. Some six months later, in order to further protect their bodies, Emma had them reburied adjacent to the Smith family cemetery near the Old Homestead.

The settlement of Joseph Smith's estate dragged on for years. There was some trouble between Emma and the Twelve regarding the distribution of property, but in spite of her personal dislike for Brigham Young, Emma was not malicious. She never would have cheated the Church to improve her own financial circumstances. Even so, she was left with the realization that she alone now was responsible for the support and education of her children.

One the 17th of November, 1844, five months after Joseph's death, Emma delivered her ninth child: a son, David Hyrum Smith. All of Nauvoo had anxiously anticipated the child's birth. Eliza R. Snow heralded little David's safe arrival with poetry:

> Sinless as celestial spirits—
> Lovely as a morning flow'r
> Comes the smiling infant stranger
> In an evil-omen'd hour
>
> Thou may'st draw from love and kindness
> All a mother can bestow;
> But alas! on earth, a father
> Thou are destin'd not to know!

In spite of the presence of children and friends, Emma was more alone now than ever before. She had her memories, and many of them were comfort to her soul, but some were not. Only God could understand her sufferings. It was a theme that was to resound over and over again in all her correspondence and interviews for the rest of her life. She did feel close to her mother-in-law, Lucy Mack Smith, and though relations were not always easy with William, her husband's only surviving brother, she did get along amiably with Joseph's sisters. But she was so lonely—and her youth was gone. She had grown prematurely old. Gradually, almost without thought, she began to replace her brighter dresses with ones of more somber hues, of plum or violet, shades more suitable to her constant spirit of mourning. Her sorrow was aggravated by unpleasant memories. Only her children—Julia, Joseph, Freddy, Alex and David—diminished her misery.

Why hadn't she lived more in happiness while she had had Joseph by her side? Had he been happy with her? She knew that he had. But could not she have made things better? During the seventeen and a half years of their marriage she and Joseph had lived in at least a dozen homes across five states. During these years, she and Joseph had buried six of their eleven children. Across these years, her greatest joy had been her love for Joseph. Could she not see, looking back, that ironically her strong loyalty to Joseph had been the cause for some of her deepest sorrow? It should have been the other way around. Now, Joseph, ever young, would remain sacred forever in her thoughts; her greatest comfort would be the assurance that she would be with him after death.

Prior to Joseph's final journey to Carthage, Emma had asked him for a special blessing. He had told her to compose the finest blessing imaginable and he would sign and sanction it upon his return. In the prospective blessing, Emma had written: "I desire with all my heart to honor and respect my husband as my head, ever to live in his confidence and by acting in unison with him retain the place which God has given me by his side."

Emma had struggled to do this. She had forsaken father and mother, home, security, and all that she owned or might ever own for Joseph. Because of her obedience and sacrifice, she had received the most exalting ordinances of the Restoration: she had been endowed and eternally sealed to Joseph, and with him at last had made her calling and election sure. Beyond the veil, Emma surely would reign as Joseph's priestess and queen.

Wedded Again

**D**ecember, 1847, marked the end of Emma's intense mourning for Joseph. Though her life was still in disorder, she was finally ready to form new attachments. She would never forget Joseph, nor could she ever ignore her witness of his divine call.

Emma was sharply criticized by those who followed Brigham Young for remaining in Illinois apart from the Church; her refusal to support the Twelve was undeniably troublesome. That the Elect Lady of Mormonism apparently rejected the most conspicuous claimants to Joseph Smith's mantle did not make the transition to new leadership any easier. But Emma's strength was in Joseph and no one else, and with Joseph gone, there was no one to follow further. What strength remained for her was in her ties to all that Joseph represented, and that was a strength indeed to be reckoned with. There was still power and authority associated with the Smith family, both dead and living. The family had been one of the major links to the Restoration. And they had remained in Nauvoo.

For Emma, moving west really was out of the question, yet, remaining in Nauvoo also presented problems. Much as she had loved Joseph and his family, she could hardly be expected to remain a widow for the rest of her life. She was terribly alone. She needed help with her children. She needed financial support. She needed protection. She needed someone to serve, someone to give organization to her life.

On the anniversary of the Prophet's birth, the 23rd of December, 1847, Emma Hale Smith was wedded a second time. The groom was a forty-three-year-old non-Mormon, "Major" Lewis Crum Bidamon, a native of Virginia. Predictably, the union provoked considerable gossip in Mormon circles, and even family friends complained that Bidamon had married Emma for her property. Church members were offended because Bidamon was not a Latter-day Saint; some thought Emma should have become a plural wife to Brigham Young, and still others thought she should have remained a widow, single-mindedly devoted to the memory of her dead husband.

But regardless of others' opinions, Emma went ahead. Lewis Bidamon answered some of her needs. He was the same age as Emma, rather handsome, well dressed, with an easy sense of humor which took few things seriously. He needed a wife, and Emma needed a husband. "You are alone," he had said when he proposed to her, "and I am alone. Let us live our lives together." Emma threw herself into her marriage to Bidamon with great abandon, almost as though she were trying to forget her past and present troubles.

For the first few years, all surviving correspondence shows that Emma did indeed come to love Lewis Bidamon. Here, at last, was the relaxation she had longed for. Life with Joseph had been so intense, so driving, so momentous. Now, with Lewis Bidamon, little mattered but the day-by-day necessities. Life was so simple. Bidamon was not ambitious. He was not trying to establish a kingdom. He was not difficult to please—and he loved her in his way, not with the intensity, the fierceness of Joseph's love, but with a matter-of-factness which was never threatening, at least at first, to her need to belong and to possess.

They made their livelihood together by the operation of the Nauvoo Mansion hotel, but there were also farms and other properties to manage. It all worked out quite well. Emma and Lewis were together until her death nearly thirty-two years later, but their romantic love must have been short-lived; his profanity, his drinking, and his infidelity progressively estranged them.

Emma almost unprotestingly put up with the "Major's" bad habits, but her tolerance could hardly hide the fact that she abhorred them. The careworn expression of Emma's face became increasingly more noticeable during her later years. She was discontented and restless, but there was no place to go.

She had few friends and no intimates. She rarely spoke of her past. The constant questioning of hotel guests about Joseph Smith and polygamy and the Church in Utah, must have contributed to her need to formulate some fixed responses. Joseph had sworn Emma to solemn secrecy about the practice of plural marriage, and the truth was certainly nothing she wanted her sons to discover. That their father had more than twenty wives at the time of his death, four of whom she herself had selected, would not reflect well upon him nor upon her. She could not allow that. Besides, had not Joseph told her that he would relinquish all for her sake? With the passage of years, Emma's denials of plural marriage became one of the falsehoods against which truth and reason had no power. The truth was simply impossible for her to admit or confess.

Western visitors passed frequently through Nauvoo. Many were Mormons who had known Emma in the days of Joseph; others who had not known Joseph were anxious to meet the widow of the martyred leader. For most of them, she was no longer "an elect lady." Her rejection of Brigham Young as Joseph's successor and her denial of Nauvoo plural marriage after its public announcement in Salt Lake City in 1852, constituted in their minds a complete repudiation of all that her first husband had died for. For them she was "apostate."

Until her death, Emma remained condescending to all outsiders, but especially to Utah Mormons. However much she might have needed real living links to her past, she remained insular and alone. Her habitual silence was often interpreted by visitors as evidence of pride and contempt. What had been for her a desire to rest, to remain in Nauvoo, to care for her children, to guard the body of her dead husband and to hold private his past, was interpreted by well-meaning Mormons as self-righteousness, creating an ill-will far deeper than any might have anticipated.

But there was more to it than this. Emma's isolation bore its own witness. Who could indeed know her history? And who indeed could ever understand her silent realizations as the lonely years passed by?

Long ago, in Joseph's powerful arms she had cried and said it was not possible for him to love others and yet love her. But now she had loved Lewis Bidamon and in the realization of his imperfections had grown to love Joseph even more. Joseph had said we would learn by our own experience. How true this was! Had she not turned angrily away from sharing Joseph in a purity and light which she had been almost forcibly brought to know was of God? She had refused the experience and the learning. Looking back now, how had she learned? Unthinkingly, she had come to love Lewis Bidamon who was far from holy, most certainly not a man of God. He was a man of the world, carnal, sensual, not faithful to his marriage vows—neither with her, nor with his two marriages before her. Nearly twenty years after marriage to Emma he had fathered a child with Nancy Abercrombie, a dark-haired, brown-eyed widow who had come alone to Nauvoo. Emma had taken the child into her home and loved him and raised him as her own—and even in time, taken the mother in also. How ironic it was that what she had rejected in light and the powers of heaven with a prophet of God, even her Joseph, she had been brought to accept alone and in the dark with a man of the world who knew no God. Rejecting the real, she had lived the counterfeit. God did indeed have a way of teaching his unwilling children their lessons. She had learned that.

Declining Years

I n the absence of a personal diary it is difficult to reconstruct Emma's activities after her second marriage. We catch glimpses of her at home in Nauvoo through other people's journals and letters, or through her own correspondence with her children, especially with Joseph, III. One by one, her grown children left her watch and care. Julia married Elisha Dixon in 1850, and went to Texas to live. After Dixon was accidentally killed by the explosion of a steamboat boiler, Julia and her little girl came back to Nauvoo where they remained until Julia's second marriage in 1857.

Emma's oldest son, Joseph, idolized his mother; the closeness is apparent in their correspondence. Even before Joseph, III's, marriage in 1856, unhappy wandering members of various splinter-groups of the Mormon Church were insisting that he affiliate with them. Although young Joseph retained some reservations, by March, 1860, he had written to William Marks that he had determined to take his "father's place as the head of the Mormon Church." On the 4th day of April, 1860, accompanied by his mother, Emma, he left Nauvoo for Amboy, Illinois. There, on the thirtieth anniversary of the organization of the Church, he was chosen and sustained president of the high priesthood and prophet, seer, and revelator to the Reorganized Church of Jesus Christ of Latter Day Saints.

Understandably, Emma did not put any pressure on him to follow this course, but after his decision she gave him her full support.

After Joseph, III, became the leader of the Reorganized Church, attempts to make Emma Smith's memory respectable among Utah Mormons were fruitless. In early 1860, Hyrum's two sons and a son of his brother Samuel, visited their Aunt Emma in Nauvoo and found her older but unchanged in mind. Hyrum's son, Joseph F., wrote that "Emma seemed very cold and distant." Very cognizant of the "missionary wandering" of her nephews, which no doubt awoke resentments from her being left alone in the past by a missionary husband, Emma had sighed, "I hope the time will come when we can all stay at home." Samuel's son, Samuel H.B., reported a puzzling strangeness about Emma that piqued his curiosity. "I think we all have our ways," he wrote, "and especially *her.*" The other son of Hyrum, John, the Presiding Patriarch of the Church in Utah, extended an invitation to Alexander to visit the Great Basin, to which Emma replied, "No child of hers would ever be permitted to go to Salt Lake." The most astute observation about Emma at this time was recorded by Samuel H.B. when he wrote that his aunt's influence concerning the Utah Church was made more profound through her silence than were she "to converse . . .personally on the subject."

Brigham Young had earlier wished for a reconcilation, but after Joseph, III, accepted the Reorganized Church's position, he made some strong remarks in public about Emma. "She is one of the damnedest liars I know of on this earth," he stated in 1866. Emma replied that Joseph had confided to her that if Brigham Young ever took the leadership of the Church he would lead it to hell. She charged President Young with "falsehoods and impious profanity," and noted that there was "not the least particle of friendship existing" between her and Brigham. The fact that both Emma and Brigham Young, in their own separate ways, loved Joseph, meant that they could never ignore one another, but their ideological positions were irreconcilably different.

Joseph, III, directed the affairs of the new church from Nauvoo until the winter of 1865 when he moved to Plano, Illinois. By then, Frederick had died, leaving a wife, Annie Maria, and a daughter, Alice Fredericka, but there was little closeness here for Emma. By 1866, Annie Maria had remarried and moved to Chicago.

Alexander had married in 1861, but soon after Joseph, III, moved to Plano, was called on a mission to Utah as a representative of the Reorganized Church. His expectant wife Lizzie and their two children, Frederick and Vida, were left in Emma's care. In 1869, David joined Alexander on a second mission to Utah. Her two sons were constantly on

Emma's mind. During their absence, she wrote regularly, fearing they might not withstand the arguments that the Utah Mormons would give them. Hard as she tried, she was unable to push these worries from her mind.

Emma was always a devoted grandparent, sharing the responsibility of rearing her grandchildren with their mothers. Alexander's family, with the exception of a few years, remained in Nauvoo until just a year before Emma's death. Emma felt particularly close to them. She had written, "If kind Heaven lets my children, or some of them live either with me or near me I shall begin to see some of the good I am living for." Emma found pure joy in her burgeoning posterity, and the perpetual chatter of such a large and exuberant family did not bother her.

After Joseph, III, moved his family to Plano, Emma anxiously awaited word from them, especially from Emma Josepha, her eldest grandchild. She was anxious to hear about their health, schooling, and projects. "It certainly does me a great good," she wrote, "let Emma write as often as she wants to . . .there are a great many parents that would be proud if not thankfull if their children, and grandchildren had the affection and talent to write them as mine do to me." Her eyesight had become poor, but she could still read through her spectacles. Her own letters were newsy, reporting of local deaths, marriages, and the progress of the Reorganized Church at Nauvoo.

Throughout her letters, Emma reaffirmed her faith in the divinity of the Restoration of the gospel, and the fact of God's purposes in the world. It was obvious that her faith was not solely dependent on rational proof. She had a witness of the spirit as well. In November, 1869, she wrote Joseph, III, "I have seen very many trying scenes in my life in which I could not see any good in them, neither could I see any place where any good could grow out of them, but yet I feel a divine trust in God, that all things shall work for good."

Emma was a model citizen. Quietly, and with reserve, she won the admiration of much of the community. At sixty-five, she was the most reliable midwife in Nauvoo—even the local physician referred hard cases to her. Emma had acquired a practical knowledge of herbs and had high regard for their therapeutic qualities.

As co-proprietor of the principal hotel in Nauvoo, her interaction with boarders kept her abreast of current affairs. The new railroads, canals, and overland routes from the East helped push Illinois' population over one million in the 1850's. The frontier was rapidly disappearing as industrialization began to move westward, but much of the state was still rural. By 1850, many Illinois towns enjoyed the telegraph, and while log cabins were fast being replaced by frame and brick houses, most towns, like

Nauvoo, still had dirt streets, and remained dependent on a community water well and pump. Most towns did not have gas lighting. Housing was scarce and expensive. Some of Emma's hotel guests remained several weeks, even months. Emma was well aware that Nauvoo had not benefited from the state's internal improvement programs. One day Emma wittingly remarked, "We must wait for Gen. [Ulysses S.] Grant to move the capital of the United States here before we have any material improvement in Nauvoo."

But Emma loved Nauvoo. She had a strong attachment to the river. Unremitting and majestic, the great Mississippi seemed to have a therapeutic effect on her. Almost free of rapids, its gentle movement across the great river valley traced the easy curve of the Nauvoo peninsula. Emma loved to watch its perpetual flow; it gave her a feeling of security. Often as she walked its shoreline, she remembered her childhood beside the shady Susquehanna. How beautiful the trees were by her father's house, leaning regally over the water, trailing low branches in the slow-moving stream. How simple everything had been then! Where oh where had all the years gone?

Emma took great pride in her gardening. She worked hard for her age. She enjoyed good health. With the exception of a broken left arm, due to a fall down the cellar stairs in the Mansion House in the summer of 1872, she was in good physical condition. Much of her day was spent in her yard. She grew all her own vegetables, and was particularly fond of her grapes and cherries. In 1867, she lamented that her gardens had produced only one third of their normal yield, and yet that year she sold nearly two hundred boxes of grapes and made over three hundred gallons of wine. Lewis regularly helped Emma in the garden, something Joseph had rarely been able to do. "I never wanted [Joseph] to go into the garden to work, " she wrote in 1870, "for if he did it would not be fifteen minutes before there would be three or four, or sometimes a half a dozen men round him and they would tramp the ground down faster than he could hoe it up."

She seldom left Nauvoo, and was perfectly satisfied to complete her life fulfilling daily chores. "I have always found enough to do to fill up all my time, " she wrote, "doing just what was very plainly and positively my duty without clamoring for some unenjoyed privilege."

With so many of her family having either been born or died in the Mansion House, its memory would always be sacred. The old frame building had caught fire many times, and Emma believed that the Lord had saved the Mansion House from burning down because it housed the manuscript of the Prophet's inspired translation of the Bible. Persistently, she had hoped that one day she would have a new house in which to live, but by 1867, she had given up the idea altogether. In December of that year, she wrote Joseph, III, that the fence around the family cemetery behind the Old Homestead was in bad repair and that she had given some thought to her place of burial. "I do not expect ever to be able to build me house to live in [but] I would like to fix a place to be put away in when I have done all my work on the earth." To her delight, however, in 1871 Lewis dismantled a large portion of the walls of the old unfinished Nauvoo House and on the southwest corner of the original foundation, erected a two-story structure over a high, dry basement. They called it the "Riverside Mansion."

For Emma, who had lived in the Mansion House for twenty-eight years, the new riverside home was an unexpected realization of a dream. She felt it fulfilled a promise she had received that her "last days should be her best." In December, 1871, she informed Joseph, III, that they had moved into their new home: "We are all well here at the river side at present. My health is better now than it has been for two years. I have not had a cold since I have lived here. We sleep up stairs all the time."

The last few years of Emma's life passed away in relative comfort. She occupied herself with sewing and minor household chores. As always, her children were ever present in her mind. Julia was having hard times in St. Louis with her second marriage. "Poor Julia has a trying life," wrote Emma in 1871. Her husband was given to excessive drinking, and was in bad health and unable to provide for his family. Julia remained with him for twenty years, but at last returned to Nauvoo two years before Emma's death.

Perhaps more disturbing to Emma though than Julia's marital problems was the deterioration of David Hyrum's mental health. He had been unwell since before his mission to Utah. David had begun to have hallucinations, and later it was discovered that he had diabetes. Finally, in January, 1877, following what was called prolonged "brain fever," David was committed to the Northern Illinois hospital for the insane. Emma described her son's condition as a "living trouble." She believed that David's missions had made his condition worse. She expressed "intense regret" that David had ever visited Salt Lake City, and insisted she had "warned him not to go." But David had gone, and had returned from Utah believing that his mother had "deceived" her children regarding Joseph and Nauvoo polygamy.

On the 30th of April, 1879, at the Riverside Mansion, at 4:20 in the morning, Emma Hale Smith Bidamon quietly and peacefully passed away. Lewis Bidamon was there, and at her bedside were her children, Julia, Joseph, III, and Alexander. She was nearly seventy-five, and old and tired. It had been a long life, much longer than she had often wanted it to be.

During the days before her death she had spoken often of the reality of life after death. She was constantly aware of Joseph's presence in the room. She said he had come to her in vision and shown her through a great "mansion of light" where she had seen and held her little baby Don Carlos, and where Joseph had promised her that she would have all her children. "Be patient," he had said, "you shall have them all." She looked forward to that. It would be good to have those little lost ones again, and her living children, and to be with her Joseph.

In her last moments, those who were with her said she seemed to be resting peacefully, then, abruptly, she raised herself up in her bed, and reached out with her left hand. "Joseph—Joseph—" she said. And then she died.

PART II

NOTEBOOK OF INTERVIEWS

Audentia Smith Anderson, *Emma's granddaughter, January 1915*
(Courtesy Doris Fredrick)

**Interviews about
Emma Hale
With Emma McC[allum]
Elbert
Fred A &c
Keep†**

*Emma Smith McCallum, Emma's granddaughter
(Courtesy Alma R. Blair)*

Emma Smith McCallum's Reminiscences*

Emma Hale & Emma McC[allum].
Rented Hotel Coffee Large Urn (Fred A.)[1]
spout & Spigot.
Kept Cookies or
Small Cakes or doughnuts
always on hand
Raised biscuits served often
lump of dough taken from
batch to start another
Salt Rising bread, too
Corn bread
every day for my breakfast
Bacon grease & molasses
(Father said)[2]
Doughnuts—twisted
Killed own pork
bought beef from butcher
nearby
[Grandmother] kept cows, made own
butter cottage "Dutch" cheese
wooden churn & dasher
Dairy house in old horse barn
had in time when [she] ran hotel
Put up so many horses
Corner part [of] stone basement[3]
divided—Kept corn there
an[d] milk. Pigs—dairy

***Emma Smith McCallum**, Emma's grand-daughter (Courtesy Doris Fredrick)*

***Joseph Smith III**, Emma's son (Courtesy LDS Church Archives)*

***"Major" Lewis C. Bidamon**, Emma's second husband (Courtesy Alma R. Blair)*

***Emmeline Griswold Smith**, Emma's daughter-in-law (Courtesy Alma R. Blair)*

hay above in big loft
3 story [building]
[Grandmother] kept milk [in] basement
of her house—The later years
Emma [McCallum] lived with her. She
hadn't cows She couldn't
milk & Major⁴ wouldn't
Emma [McCallum] used to help milk
Old Brindle a gentle
cow—[Emma McCallum] lived with her
[Grandmother] before the family left Nauvoo⁵
no hired man
several cows
[Grandmother] used to weave but
not in Emma's [McCallum] day.
Had several spreads
blue & white, & pink &
white woven. But perhaps
not [made] by her
[Grandmother] made her own dresses
Rather low in neck—always
wore a white collar
or three cornered piece
of white—neckerchief
thin cloth—plain
Dresses rather long waisted
tall woman,⁶ full skirts
gather ad[ded] on.
Didn't go out very
much. Buried in
a rather dark—brocaded
flowers raised—sort of
<u>plum</u> color [dress]⁷
Black riding habit but gave
up riding before old age
Bonnet with veil but

Emma and David Hyrum Smith, *from daguerreotype (reverse image) circa 1845*
(Courtesy Lynn E. Smith)

ribbon or string—thrown
back partly brim
never saw her wear
it over face—tied
under chin[8]
[Grandmother] <u>always</u> wore choker [of] gold
beads, not gradated
never saw her without
beads. She gave beads
to Emma [McCallum the] last time Emma [McCallum]
was there before Emma [McCallum]
married.[9] Beads had
broken & lost some—
She had filled out with
ambers.
Never saw her wear
the <u>watch</u>.[10]
When [Emma McCallum was] a child Gr[andmother] kept
it in a drawer of dresser[11] [which]
Elbert[12] has got. Emma [McCallum]
used to go & look at [it]
there & saw watch.
Elbert has Gr[and]f[ather Smith's] leather dressing
case—razor—
shave brush
Stick pin or breastpin
used to fasten collar
Locks of hair in pin[13]
Go often am[on]g sick
but didn't dress up to
go out—Emma [McCallum] can't
remember.
[Grandmother was] healthy all life
not quick [of] motion
but [could] get around & do more
work in a day than most

The Nauvoo House or Riverside Mansion, circa 1871
(*Courtesy Audry Guetzow*)

others.
[In] later years [she] did all
her own work. Washing &
all, no machine.
[Emma McCallum] remembers no carpets
at Riverside Mansion[14]
<u>parlor</u> had a carpet
Mansion House[15] [had] bare
floors.
She [Grandmother] fell in Mansion House
Maj. B[idamon]. had two large
vineyards. [He] made [a]lot of
wine. [He] made stair steps
to cellar wide—to put
barrels of wine. She took
milk &c up & down to keep
cool. She fell & broke
[her] work arm—may not have been
set right or had to
use it too soon—crooked
<u>bent</u> not twisted.[16]
<u>Great</u> cabinet in <u>Kitchen</u>
drawers in front—table [to]
wash dishes, Kneaded
bread &c—had to <u>clear</u> a
Garden—some flowers
in back yard—sandy
not good for flowers
nice vegetable garden
on right of Mansion
House both Emma & Gr[andpa Bidamon]
worked.
(Radishes)
Everything grew for her:
pot[atoes], onions, turnips
cabbage—[She] put in cellar

The Mansion House or Nauvoo Mansion, circa 1900, foreground Heman C. Smith and Vida Smith Smith, Emma's granddaughter and husband (Courtesy Earlita Inslee)

grapes—pick & she would
put wax on end of
bunch—hang in cellar
in cool place have
grapes nearly all winter.
[Grandmother] tall—large frame
ingenue in prime, large,
erect in youth
stooped in old age was
thin
Brunette.
not unduly wrinkled
but took no care to
preserve skin.
sheep tallow for chaped
hands.
She didn't talk much
Kept th[ou]g[ht]s to herself. Heard
her speak to her bro David [Hale][17]
He came to visit her
[David was the] only one Emma [McCallum] ever saw
[that] resembled her [i.e., Grandmother]—tall—
dark, dark eyes—
[In the] fall have whole string
of dif[ferent] herbs tied up
to dry & cure. Made a
salve—Every body knew
of Mother Bidamon's salves
for cuts—bruises—fever—
rheumatism—for every
kind of ache & pain.
Tonic made of herbs
Saffron—spearmint,
catnip—
[Grandmother] always had a herd
of cats—dozens of

Joseph Smith, III, Emma's son, circa 1860 (Courtesy Audio-Visual Department, Reorganized Church of Jesus Christ of Latter Day Saints)

them. When
she'd go to milk she'd
milk in pans for cats
Twice a day get fill—
Kept barn clear of
mice & rats.
Capnip tea & they'd
lap it up.
<u>Mend</u> little Joseph's[18]
coat of many colors
Knitt[in]g lying on table
all time—sit to read
she'd Knit
Necessities in house
but no luxuries or
handsome furnishing.
Perhaps in Gr[andfather Joseph Smith's] day had
better. tore back part of
Hotel off[19]—2 rooms
up stairs fitted very
beautifuly—4 poster
bed—closet [and] secret place[20]
10 bedrooms [were in the] back
[Each room was] small—[with] bed, wash
stand & chair
over di[nin]g room & Kitchen
Parlor—doormat lovely rug &
pictures—[Emma McCallum] can't remember
curtains—lace or not
but drapes of <u>silk</u>
of maroon heavy &
brocaded if she
remembers correctly.
Furniture wonderful
also. Windsor chair
[Grandmother was] up at 4 o'c in summer

Julia Murdock Smith Dixon Middleton, *Emma's adopted daughter (Courtesy Audio-Visual Department, Reorganized Church of Jesus Christ of Latter Day Saints)*

break of day—
trudge to barn to
milk bef[ore]. break[fast]—
Maj[or Bidamon].—bed, snoring.
No [harsh] words—He took
care of money end—She
pay bills—Bar room[21]
liquor—cards—drunk
vomit—on bed clothes
& girls had to clean it
up—He was friend of
Mormons[22]—fine looking
[but] very profane—She
suffered so much—she
needed a protector[23]
Good housekeeper.
very clean—
Had no time to read
Sit down to read—fall
asleep—Read good
deal in younger life
Father[24] took Chicago Tribune
for her for years
to time of her death
She had Herald after
it was started.[25]
Go to church.
Rem[em]bers hearing how [she] moved plates of
B[ook] of M[ormon] when dusting
Hid them in barrel of
beans once[26]
Julia [Murdock Smith] the lady[27]—didn't
wash dishes or other
hard work. Proud
selfish.
[Grandmother would] visit with neighbors [who] came

(L-R) **Zaide Smith Salyards, Carrie Smith Weld and Emma Smith McCallum**, *Emma's granddaughters (Author's collection)*

in.
Sing about her work
(very clear high sop[rano].)[28]
No musical instruments
many friends—
Always could talk to any
one no matter who.
Hundreds of people visit
the old Mormon town during
Emma's [McCallum] stay in Nauvoo[29]
[Visitors would] ask to see Grandmother
always wore apron
standing talking, turn
her apron up at
corners & finger it—
talk to men & women
of all walks of life
drs. lawyers—everybody [asked]
before [they] left—Did
your husb[and] practice
polyg[amy]—did he have
more wives than
you? "No—I am
the only wife he ever
had"—died with it on
her lips[30]—E.L. Kelly
took [the] same testimony[31]
~~Reaffirmed~~
[Grandmother] abhorred polyg[amy]—can
see her yet as she'd
stand up & denounce
the charge of polyg[amy].
She was of iron will
truthfulness—If Jos[eph]
had had anyth[ing] to do
with polyg[amy]—she

(Seated) Joseph Smith, III. (Standing L-R) Lucy Smith Lysinger, Hale Washington Smith, Israel Alexander Smith, Frederick Madison Smith and Audentia Smith Anderson, Emma's son and grandchildren (Author's collection)

would not [have stood] by him
or all the years [she] testif[ied]
to a lie[32]
She was hated
because of this stand—
[She was] of sufic[ient] inteligence
Strict with [the] children
Didn't spare the rod
[Emma McCallum] heard [her] father say so—[33]
[Grandmother's] four boys slept in
room off hers—to
guard them.[34]
I used to sleep there.
Father[35] punished me
for running away
because I wanted to be
with grandmother Smith
Loved her better than
my own mother,[36] who
was frail, & had other
children, & gr[mother]
took great deal of care
fed me, put me to
sleep [and said]—let her stay
there—
[Grandmother had] sense of humor
if not, [she would have] gone <u>under</u>
Dignified—jolly
loved a joke—
but <u>dignified</u> not
proud—had mind of
her own. When she
got up & left childr[en] in
Plano [Illinois], & Emeline [Griswold Smith][37]
went out with her
some remark father [i.e., Joseph Smith, III]

*Scene from **Hamlet** by **David Hyrum Smith**,
Emma's son (Courtesy Audio-Visual Department, Reorganized Church of Jesus Christ
of Latter Day Saints)*

*Nativity scene by **David Hyrum Smith**, Emma's
son (Courtesy Audio-Visual Department,
Reorganized Church of Jesus Christ of
Latter Day Saints)*

*(L-R) **Alexander Hale Smith and David Hyrum Smith**, Emma's sons
(Courtesy Lynn E. Smith)*

made—[Grandmother] got into
the quorum's pews
set apart for elders—[38]

———————

Indignant when
they had a man &
woman who wanted
a room in hotel—
Major gave bed
room off from stairs
In nite terrible
moaning hollering
Maj[or] investigated
both drunk &
threw [up] in bed—mess
to clean up. He
made them go in
middle of nite
it mottled—
Uncle David [Hyrum Smith] always
drew pictures—[39]
[Grandmother] bitter against Utah [Church]
never wore earrings
never wore hoopskirts
[Would] get angry but had
control—poised.
Candles
made—buy mutton tallow
& wicks hung on
few wires
Lamps
—moulds—
boarders took candles
to room—every day
Emma Mc[Callum] had to

Emma Smith Bidamon, in later years
(Courtesy LDS Church Archives)

David Hyrum Smith and Clara C. Hartshorn,
Emma's son and Daughter-in law, wedding day,
10 May 1870 (Courtesy Lynn E. Smith)

Joseph Smith III, Emma's son
(Author's collection)

Emma Smith McCallum, Emma's granddaughter (Author's collection)

clean candlesticks
scrape off the
melted tallow
& put new wick
[Grandmother] had some beautiful
tall brass [candle]sticks
[Her] hair parted in middle
Rolls over ear—caught
by comb—long curls
put in [with] comb[40]
Shoulder shawl
of silk[41]—when dressed
up—
Fireplaces for
heat—cook stove
shoulder shawl of
wool if cool—
Paisley shawl
Spin yarn
had wheel—
dye hanks
tie strings many
places—in Knitt[ing]
tied plaits &c white red
blue—to match
Served children, agued,
[medicinal] beer
A stitch in time
saves nine.[42]
[Grandmother was] very affectionate
in memory of Grfather [Joseph Smith]
[Major] Bidamon a strength
& intelligent—pleasing
personality but
got to drinking
—woman visits too.

Emma Smith Bidamon, *(photograph retouched) (Courtesy Audio-Visual Department, Reorganized Church of Jesus Christ of Latter Day Saints)*

who lived near
[Nancy] Abercrombie[43]
Major Lewis Bidamon
[Charles] Edward [Bidamon]—child [was]
about 7 [when Grandmother] <u>adopted</u>[44]

Charles Edward Bidamon, *Emma's "stepson"*
(Courtesy Ruth Brown)

NOTES FOR
Emma Smith McCallum's Reminiscences

†Mary Audentia Smith Anderson, Emma Hale Smith's grandchild, was the daughter of Joseph Smith, III, and Bertha Madison. Born 23 March 1872 at Plano, Illinois, she married Benjamin M. Anderson (24 February 1891) and they were the parents of seven children. An avid genealogist and a prodigious researcher, Audentia compiled and published an exhaustive history of the Smith family: *Ancestry and Posterity of Joseph Smith and Emma Hale* (Independence: Herald Publishing House, 1929). She died at Independence on 5 May 1963. The following interview notes were taken by Audentia Anderson prior to the publication of her work on the Smith family. The notebook is now owned by Audentia's grandson, H.G. "Bud" Fredrick.

*Emma Josepha Smith McCallum (1857-1940) was Emma Hale Smith's first grandchild. Born in Nauvoo on 28 July 1857, she was the daughter of Joseph Smith, III, and Emmeline Griswold. She married Alexander McCallum at Plano, Illinois, 1 January 1875, and they were the parents of four children. She died 30 November 1940 at Lamoni, Iowa.

1. The hotel referred to is the Nauvoo Mansion House. Emma Hale Smith's grandson, Frederick Alexander Smith (1862-1954), was the eldest child of Alexander Hale Smith and Elizabeth Agnes Kendall. Emma McCallum is most probably remembering her early childhood in Nauvoo during the time that Fred A. Smith's father, Alexander, rented the Mansion House.

2. Emma McCallum's father was Joseph Smith, III, first surviving son of Emma Hale and Joseph Smith. Born 6 November 1832, in Kirtland, Ohio, he was nearly twelve years old at the time of his father's death. He married three times: Emmeline Griswold (22 October 1856) by whom he fathered five children. Shortly after Emmeline's death, he married Bertha Madison (12 November 1869) and they were the parents of nine children. Following Bertha's accidental death in 1896, Joseph, III, married Ada Rachel Clark (12 January 1898) by whom he fathered three sons.

3. The text refers to the stone basement of the old horsebarn which was located immediately east of the Mansion House. The barn was a "large and commodious" brick structure, adequate to stable seventy-five horses.

4. "Major" Lewis Crum Bidamon, a native of Virginia, was born 16 January 1804. Bidamon's first wife, Nancy Sebree, died in 1827, and his 1842 marriage to Mary Ann Douglas ended in failure. The non-Mormon widower, accused of marrying for property, was wedded to Emma Hale Smith on 23 December 1847. Although he tried his luck in the California gold fields in 1849, Nauvoo remained his permanent residence until his death on 11 February 1891.

5. Joseph Smith, III, with his family left Nauvoo in the winter of 1865-66 to become editor of the *Saints' Herald* (the official organ of the RLDS Church) in Plano, Illinois.

6. Emma Hale Smith was often referred to as a tall, large woman, possibly measuring five feet seven or eight inches in height. Samuel O. Bennion, who viewed Emma's skeletal remains in January 1928, observed: "She must have been quite a large woman, because the bones in her legs were almost as long as the leg bones of the skeletons of Joseph and Hyrum" (Samuel O. Bennion to Heber J. Grant and Counselors, 21 January 1928, Church Archives).

7. A similar description of Emma Hale Smith's burial clothing was given by Audentia Anderson to Vesta Crawford: "She was buried in a rather dark dress of plum or magenta shade, brocaded with flowers and leaves in a raised design" (Vesta Crawford Notes, J. Willard Marriott Library, Manuscripts Division, University of Utah. Hereafter cited as Vesta Crawford Notes).

8. "Her riding dress was black with a bonnet of a sort of poke style with which she wore a vale which could be pulled back to expose the face. Her riding whip had an ivory handle and her side-saddle was also very elegant" (Vesta Crawford Notes).

9. Emma McCallum married in 1875 (see asterisked footnote above). Audentia informed Vesta Crawford that "Emma had a string of gold beads all the same size, real yellow gold and they fitted her neck rather closely, she wore them until there were holes in some of them, and they were flattened and bent" (Vesta Crawford Notes).

10. The watch referred to, possibly a gift from a Church convert, had been sent to Emma Hale Smith from England.

11. The dresser referred to is now in the possession of Lynn Elbert Smith of Independence, Missouri. The four-drawer highboy in Emma's bedroom was colonial style with curved legs. A huge deep drawer at the top was opened by the bottom part that protruded over the other three drawers. The lower drawers were opened by flat knob handles. The mirror above the dresser was detached and framed in plain mohagony to match the dresser. Resting on top of the dresser was the Prophet's little dressing case which contained a razor, strop, combs, brushes, jars for salves, and a pair of "pulls" for boots. The handles of the pulls were made into a button-hook and a screwdriver.

12. Elbert Aoriul Smith (1871-1959), Emma Hale Smith's grandson, was the only child of David Hyrum Smith and Clara Charlotte Hartshorn. He is the father of Lynn Elbert Smith mentioned in note 11.

13. Under Emma's supervision, the bodies of Joseph and Hyrum Smith were disinterred and reburied in a secret location about six months after the martyrdom. At that time, Emma obtained a lock of hair from each of the martyrs' heads which she secured in a broach.

14. The Riverside Mansion was formerly known as the Nauvoo House. Lewis C. Bidamon dismantled a large portion of the walls of the unfinished Nauvoo House and erected a two-story structure on the southwest corner of the original foundation. It was used as a residence by the family beginning in 1871.

15. The Mansion House was located across the street from the "Old Homestead." Completed in September 1843, the large house comfortably accommodated the Prophet's six-member family and also served as a hotel.

16. The accident was reported in the *Deseret News* 21 (21 August 1872):425: "Emma had her arm in a sling, having fallen down the cellar quite recently and broken her left arm just above the wrist, which she said was doing well" (Edward Stevenson to *Deseret News*, 9 August 1872, Cincinnati, Ohio).

17. Emma Hale Smith's brother, David Hale (born 6 March 1794), was the second child of Isaac Hale and Elizabeth Lewis. He and others of Emma's immediate family had settled in Lee County, Illinois, in the late

1830s and early 1840s. The visit of David Hale, referred to in the text, undoubtedly occurred in 1871, following a visit to his younger brother, Reuben, in Missouri.

18. Joseph Smith, III. The coat was so called because it had been patched and mended many times.

19. During the summer of 1890, eleven years after Emma Hale Smith's death, the east wing of the Mansion House was razed. The ten hotel rooms were located upstairs in the east wing.

20. The "secret place," located upstairs behind a panel in the closet of the northwest bedroom, served as either a hiding place or as an escape to the attic.

21. Although Emma did not allow the Prophet to equip the Mansion House with a bar (to accommodate non-Mormon hotel guests), "Major" Bidamon appears to have been patronized in this regard (see *Saints' Herald*, 22 January 1935).

22. Non-Mormons who were friendly to the Mormon Church were called "Jack Mormons" in the nineteenth century.

23. Lewis C. Bidamon was not an active member of any Christian church. While Smith family descendants have viewed Emma's marriage to Bidamon with indifference and as one of expediency, Utah Mormons traditionally have written of the union with contempt. Although the "Major" may have had a limited imagination about what to do with his time, he clearly filled a void in Emma's life and extant letters from Emma to Lewis indicate that she did love the man. Twenty-two-year-old missionary Junius F. Wells visited Nauvoo in 1876 and penned his own appraisal of Lewis Bidamon: "We also called at Nauvoo house and had dinner. When we went in we found Bidamon the proprietor & Emma Smith's husband, playing cards. He is a full robust, idle, trickly, dirty, specimen of the *homo genus*, who on short acquaintance was familiarly impudent. No one would think of taking offence from his conduct, he is so manifestly a plebeian of the lower sort" (Journal of Junius F. Wells, 21 April 1876, Church Archives).

24. Joseph Smith, III.

25. The *Saints' Herald*, official organ of the RLDS Church, has continued uninterrupted from 1860 to the present.

26. When Emma and Joseph Smith moved from Manchester, New York, to Harmony, Pennsylvania, in December 1827, the gold plates and breastplate were secreted in a barrel of beans. Lucy Mack Smith remembered the essential details of this protective measure: "The Record and breastplate for security, he [Joseph] nailed up in a box and then put them into a strong cask; and after filling the cask with beans, headed it up again" (Lucy Mack Smith, *Biographical Sketches of Joseph Smith the Prophet, and his Progenitors for Many Generations* [Liverpool: Published for Orson Pratt by S.W. Richards, 1853], p. 113).

27. Julia Murdock Smith, the adopted daughter of Emma and Joseph Smith, was born 1 May 1831 in Orange, Ohio, to John Murdock and Julia Clapp. She remained with Emma until 1850 when she married Elisha Dixon. After Dixon's tragic death, Julia returned to live with Emma in Nauvoo until about 1857 when she married John Middleton. This marriage failed and Julia again returned to Nauvoo where she remained until Emma's death in 1879. Emma McCallum is undoubtedly remembering Julia's unwillingness to help with household chores after the failure of her second marriage. Julia, who had been named for her natural mother, had resented the fact that she was adopted, but did not learn the names of her true parents until maturity. "Mine has been no easy life," she wrote her brother, John Riggs Murdock, in 1858, "[Why] could [I] not have been raised with my own blood and kin and not with strangers and bear a name I had not claim to"? It was not that Emma and Joseph had been remiss in their parental duties, for Julia declared: "[Emma] has been more than a mother to me and loves me as one of her own." Rather it was the social stigma that adoption often brings and the fact that some believed "Joseph Smith was [her] father but that [her] mother was some unfortunate girl that was betrayed by him" (Julia Murdock Smith Dixon Middleton to John Riggs Murdock, 2 November 1858, cited in Journal of John Murdock, under date, Special Collections, Harold B. Lee Library, Brigham Young University). In January 1859 Julia's natural father, John Murdock of Lehi, Utah, read her letter with much interest. Moved by compassion and some guilt, he thanked Julia for the expression of her candid feelings and invited her and spouse to come to Utah to get acquainted. Aware that Julia had been baptized a Catholic to satisfy her second husband, the elder Murdock penned a lengthy letter detailing his conversion to the Church, his witness of its divinity, and recounted his reasons for giving Julia and Joseph, her twin brother, to Emma and Joseph Smith. The mother of the twins having died when they were only six hours old, and being alone with five small children, John Murdock looked for someone to take the newborns. Because his dead wife's family was opposed to the Restoration John

consented to a request from Emma and Joseph: "Sister [Emma] Smith your foster-mother had two children [die about the same time and Joseph] sent word to me that he would take the children and raise them and also sent a man and woman for them and I sent them to him . . . . When I afterwards went to Kirtland Sister Smith requested me not to make myself known to the children as being their father: It was a hard request [but] she wanted to bring the children up as her own and never have them know anything to the contrary that they might be perfectly happy with her as their mother . . . . Joseph told me it would one day all come to light which it appears has taken place without my divulging it for I have always held my peace upon the subject" (John Murdock to Julia Murdock Smith Dixon Middleton, 20 January 1859, cited in Journal of John Murdock, under date, Special Collections, Harold B. Lee Library, Brigham Young University). There is no evidence that Julia ever came to Utah to see her father, John Murdock. (See also Joseph Smith, III, to E. L. Kelley, 7 August 1884, RLDS Library-Archives, for a short synopsis of Julia's life.)

28. Charles Derry, who characterized Emma Hale Smith as a "noble specimen of true womanhood," also declared: "She is a good singer" (Diary of Charles Derry, December 1862, RLDS Library-Archives).

29. Emma Smith McCallum left Nauvoo with her parents in the winter of 1865-66.

30. Less than three months before Emma Hale Smith's death, she purportedly stated that the Prophet Joseph Smith had never practiced plural marriage or spiritual wifery and that she had never seen a revelation regarding this doctrine or practice during the Prophet's life-time. Her testimony was published posthumously. (See *The History of the Reorganized Church of Jesus Christ of Latter Day Saints, 1844-1872* [Independence: Herald Publishing House, 1896], 3:355-56.)

31. Edmund Levi Kelley, born 17 November 1844 in Illinois, was converted to the RLDS Church in May 1864. A talented lawyer, he was appointed Presiding Bishop of the RLDS Church in 1891 and also acted as president of the Herald Publishing House. He served as a counselor to the RLDS First Presidency from 1897 to 1902 and died 10 May 1930 in Independence, Missouri.

32. Emma Smith's seeming denial of her husband's involvement in plural marriage has resulted in a long-standing controversy between members of the LDS and RLDS churches. An overwhelming prepon-

derance of evidence attests to the Prophet Joseph Smith's having taught and practiced the ancient doctrine. Similarly, Emma's repugnance to plural marriage has been copiously documented. Her decision to repudiate the existence of plurality of wives in Nauvoo (1841-44) was based upon the fact that Joseph Smith had sworn her to total secrecy regarding the practice, and by keeping that vow (after the martyrdom) she had a way out of a terribly uncomfortable situation. Also, it seems clear that from information then available to her, Emma Smith had erroneously concluded that Joseph had ceased his involvement in polygamy before his death. It is obvious by her consistent repudiation of Nauvoo plural marriage that Emma was not attempting to reject her husband's divine call, but to protect his character from those who could not possibly understand his purposes in the matter. Emma's spoken and unspoken denials of the Prophet's polygamous relationships succeeded in convincing her immediate family and, to some degree, the public that he did not teach or practice the doctrine. However, it was less easy to convince those who were personally knowing of all the ramifications of Nauvoo plural marriage during Joseph Smith's life-time. (Witness William Clayton's diary entires for 12 July and 16 August 1843.) For example, Joseph W. Coolidge reported to Joseph F. Smith a conversation he had with Emma about 1846 regarding Nauvoo polygamy. Emma remarked to Coolidge that "Joseph had abandoned plurality of wives before his death." Coolidge, family friend and administrator of the Prophet's estate, indicated that he had personal knowledge that the Mormon leader had not discontinued the ancient practice. "[Emma] insisted that he had, Coolidge insisted that he had not, for he [Coolidge] 'knew better.'" Emma Smith retorted with exasperation, "Then he was worthy of the death he died" (Diary of Joseph F. Smith, 28 August 1870, Church Archives). Emma's niece, Lovina Smith Walker, eldest child of Hyrum Smith, testified that the "Elect Lady" had openly confided certain facts regarding Joseph's marriage to additional women: "While I was living with Aunt Emma Smith in Fulton City, Fulton Co., Illinois, in the year 1846 . . .she told me that she, Emma Smith, was present and witnessed the marrying or sealing of Eliza Partridge, Emily Partridge, Maria Lawrence and Sarah Lawrence to her husband, Joseph Smith, and that she gave her consent thereto" (see Joseph Fielding Smith, *Blood Atonment and the Origin of Plural Marriage* [Independence: Zion's Printing and Publishing Co., 1905], p. 73).

33. Emma Smith McCallum's father was Joseph Smith, III.

34. Emma Hale Smith's desire to "guard" her sons was only natural. Stories of a plot to kill all members of the Smith family were widely

circulated in the wake of the Prophet's death. In 1866 Emma wrote: "No one knows the solid heartfelt pleasure I take in comparing my sons with others, and them too that has had fathers of their own to guard them" (Emma Bidamon to Joseph Smith, III, 2-3 February 1866, RLDS Library-Archives). Emma's son, David Hyrum Smith, captured in poetry his mother's concern for her children's spiritual and physical safety:

> Remember how she taught us five
> In faithfulness to pray
> That God would guard us through the night
> And watch us through the day

(Diary of David Hyrum Smith [1853-1864], 17 February [1862], "An Appeal to my Brother Frederick When on his sick bed," RLDS Library-Archives.)

35. Joseph Smith, III.

36. Emmeline Griswold Smith.

37. Emmeline Griswold Smith was Emma McCallum's mother and first wife of Joseph Smith, III.

38. The text refers to a time (after 1869) when Emma Bidamon attended church service in the RLDS meetinghouse at Plano, Illinois. Affectionately referred to as "Joseph, III's church home," the large, stone "Plano Church" was commenced in 1867 and completed for the April RLDS conference in 1869. It was the first meetinghouse completed by the RLDS Church. On the occasion referred to, Emma Hale Smith became irate when her son, Joseph, III, informed her that she had taken a seat on one of the pews designated for the priesthood. Instead of relocating, Emma stormed from the building. Of course this embarrassing incident threatened the harmony which had existed between Emma and Joseph, III. Possibly referring to this difficulty, David Hyrum Smith wrote: "It is gone Mother that unity that existed between you and Joseph" (David Hyrum Smith to Emma Bidamon, circa 1873-1876, private collection of the author).

39. David Hyrum Smith, son of Emma Hale and Joseph Smith, was born in the Mansion House on 17 November 1844, five months after the death of his father. Although well known as an artist, David was also a poet, musician and playwright. On 10 May 1870 he married Clara Charlotte

Hartshorn and they were the parents of one son. David died 29 August 1904 in Elgin, Illinois.

40. Note the use of hair combs in the painting of Emma on page 143.

41. Emma was fond of shoulder shawls. At least one of her dressy shawls is still in existence. See photographs on pages 74, 90 and 94.

42. Emma was a very practical and resourceful woman and she treated frontier illnesses in typical nineteenth-century fashion.

43. Lewis C. Bidamon's marital infidelity resulted in the birth of at least one illegitimate child: Charles Edward Bidamon. The child's mother was Nancy Perriman Brooks Abercrombie. Born about 1830, Nancy first married William H. Brooks and later a Mr. Abercrombie. It is a credit to Emma's generosity and long-suffering that she was willing to allow the child and mother into her home. Following Emma's deathbed request that the "Major" marry the child's mother, Lewis C. Bidamon and Nancy Ambercrombie were married (28 May 1880). After the "Major's" death (11 February 1891), Nancy moved to Kansas City, Missouri, where she died 30 July 1903. (See statement of William B. Brooks, Jr., 25 December 1977, Church Archives.)

44. Charles Edward Bidamon, son of Lewis Crum Bidamon and Nancy Perriman Brooks Abercrombie, was born 16 March 1864. At Nancy's urgent request, the illegitimate child was "adopted" into Emma's home. Charles penned the following tribute to Emma:

> I was taken into the home of Emma Smith Bidamon in 1868, at the age of four years, and was considered as one of the family up to and including the year of her death in 1879.
> As to my recollection of her, she was a person of very even temper. I never heard her say an unkind word, or raise her voice in anger or contention.
> She was loved and respected by the entire community, (all who knew her). And at her funeral, which the whole countryside attended, many tears flowed, showing grief at her passing. She had a queenly bearing without the arrogance of a queen. A noble woman, showing and living a charity for all. Loving and beloved . . . .
> Her children and grandchildren visited her ofttimes and loved and esteemed her highly. But I was there continually from the age of four in 1868 until her death in 1879, a period of eleven years. I should

know her disposition and character thoroughly. Her ideals were high and her disposition kindly" (Charles E. Bidamon to Warren L. Van Dine, 9 September 1940, copy of original gifted to author by Charles E. Bidamon's daughter, Leah McLean).

Although Emma had severed her ties with the Church in Utah, many viewed her actions in giving a home to the child with amazement. For example, Joseph C. Rich wrote the following to Edward Hunter from Carthage, Illinois, on Christmas Day in 1869: "[Emma] is the wife of a man who, even among his friends is reproached as a drunkard and an adulterer. Only recently an illegitimate child has been sent him, that calls Emma grandmother" (*Deseret Evening News*, 7 January 1870).

Frederick Alexander Smith, *Emma's grandson*
(Courtesy Winsome McDonald)

Frederick Alexander Smith's Reminiscences*

Fred A—
[Grandmother] wonderful—dignified
humble [a woman] as you ever met—
superior intelligence—limited
education but more than Grf[ather Joseph Smith]
lived where more privileges
prob[ably] less than High School
or acadamy, perhaps
a little.
Some books—read some
—burden.
Incident—[about Grandmother's] diplomatic
nature Fred A [got] in [a]
fight [at] school
said noth[in]g (laughed) knew if he
told it [to his] folks [he would get] scolded—
[His] mother [would have] shook him up
—Grm[other] got hold of it
[Fred A.] thot more of Grm[other] than
anyone on earth, didn't
want her to hear of it
in aft[ernoon], after work
done—[Grandmother would] sit down to
a table—& comb her
hair—side combs
aft[er a while] Fred came [to] her "I want

Arthur Marion Smith, Emma's grandson
(Courtesy Carl K. Smith)

(Sitting L-R) **Frederick Alexander Smith and Alexander Hale Smith**
(Standing L-R) **Joseph George Smith, Don Alvin Smith and Arthur
Marion Smith**, Emma's son and grandsons *(Author's collection)*

to talk"—pulled
stool up to knee.
[She] said noth[in]g all [the time] knowing
of his fight—but [she]
told of evils in world, of earthly
passions, gave nice
rebuke without refering
to his fight, [the point was] emphasized
strongly—no scold[in]g
[Fred A. was] par[ticularly] conscious
of his error—
[This helped] him better
than all scolding
Arthur [Marion Smith] (father's son)[45]
very sick—administering
not faith to [be] heal[ed]
Grm[other] finally said
Joseph[46] why don't you let
that boy go? You
haven't faith to be
heal[e]d—submit
—let Lord take
child if it's His
will &c Struck
Alex[ander] & Jos[eph. III] forcibly
& made them think
he might be holding
him here.
If you feel that
way I'll change
my tactics.
Prayed he'd go
without suffering
[Grandmother was] tall, well proportioned
straight as [an] arrow
walked dignified

Emma Smith Bidamon*, Nauvoo senior citizen (Courtesy Audio-Visual Department, Reorganized Church of Jesus Christ of Latter Day Saints)*

not arrogant
social, friendly
Many came to Hotel
wanted inf[ormation] of Prophet
Joseph, took [them] into [Grandmother's]
room—she [was] cordial [and]
civil—ans[wered] ques[tions]
"How many wives
did your husband have?"
Stiffened up—quite
dignified—"He had no
other wife than me."[47]
Friend to all & all
friend to her. Church
people very friendly
she'd gather them
in—no distinction
as to standing
democratic—<u>fair</u>
around house [Grandmother wore] dark
grey calico with little
figures, for street
[she] always [dressed] in black.
[She wore a] cloak or <u>cape</u>
voluminous—to knees
broadcloth, neat,
lined, handsome.
[Her] hair [was] <u>always</u> neat.
neat in clothing.
Exceptionall cook
made some of her
own clothing. Knit
[her] own sox
A woman used to come
& help her sew—
Sister <u>Revell</u>[48]

Alexander Hale Smith, Emma's son
(Courtesy Glenna Henderson)

[Grandmother] loved music—
[she] sang—had melodeon
Uncle David [Hyrum Smith] used
to play—but she
never touched [it]
[Grandmother would] sing hymns—
every ev[enin]g—not [need to]
light lamp—[to] sing [because she knew words]
by heart. <u>Lead</u> the
singing. Made selection
of hymns from other
churches. Printed [hymns from her]
old church—some [that were]
in existence.[49]
[Grandmother was a] horsewoman [wore a] black
rid[in]g habit—bonnet.
[Had] ivory handled [riding crop][50]
~~earrings~~[51]
<u>ring</u>[52]
Made very little reference
to any persecutions. Heard
her tell about the mob
in Hiram, O[hio].
She [was in] terror, prayed, never
expected to see him again.[53]
Reticent about tradgedy
of 1844.[54] [Viewing of] bodies in
[Mansion House] din[in]g room.[55] Buried
them in [Nauvoo House] cellar at
night—6 mons
moved to family cemetary.[56]
She told her sons where
they were—[Marked by] lilac bush
Her grave—brick wall [vault].[57]
[Martyrs bodies moved from] cellar to old spring house.
Wood house—chips

Emma Smith Bidamon, *after second marriage (Courtesy Alma R. Blair)*

(L-R) *Alexander Hale Smith and Joseph Smith, III*, *Emma's sons, 1901 (Author's collection)*

(Sitting L-R) "*Major*" *Lewis C. Bidamon, Frederick Granger Williams Smith, and Joseph Smith, III.* *(Standing L-R)* *David Hyrum Smith and Alexander Hale Smith*, *Emma's sons and her second husband, circa 1860 (Courtesy Audio-Visual Department, Reorganized Church of Jesus Christ of Latter Day Saints)*

all over gr[ound]—raked
chips away—took
surplus dirt & dumped
in river—raked
chips back—
brick house 10 × 12[58]
[Grandmother's] saddle—unusally
handsome.
[Wore] breakfast shawl
over shoulders.
Coffee—
Substantial cooking
pastries—pies
cookies, doughnuts
old urn for
doughnuts[59]
chickens—
Fred was <u>14</u> when he left Nauvoo[60]
[Grandmother was] strict—required
obed[ience]—firm but
diplomatic.
Not given to slang—
very particular in
her speech—good
construction. Write
<u>letters</u> about all
Deeply religious
—believed in B[ook] of M[ormon]—very
loyal to church.[61]
Maj. belonged to no
church but he
defended <u>her</u> &
her church.
[She] enjoyed cooking
but often retired to
own room to be quiet

Joseph Smith, III, Emma's son
(Courtesy LDS Church Archives)

& <u>alone</u> in p.m.
People came & talked about
religion—She insisted
grf[ather Joseph Smith] design[ated] Joseph [Smith, III] as
successor.[62]
[Some] tried to coax her to
go West—threatened
her—went to Fulton
City to escape—[63]
cook over open fire
in firepl[ace, with a]
crane [to hold the kettle]—
roast her
meat in kettle with
cover—
Candles—
[Grandmother] doctored own children
understood herbs
made salve[64]
of jimpson weed
beeswax mutton
tallow &c. d[octo]r sons
cuts—Fred hated smell
of jimson weed but
had to gather it.
Peop[le] came to ask
her what to do for
fever &c.—babies—
Family doctor Hamilton[65]
at Nauvoo—[parents of] little tiny
baby—He would tell
them to go to see Mrs
Bidamon she knows more
abt babies than I do.
Many mothers came
to ask. He used to

Frederick Alexander Smith, Emma's grandson
(Courtesy Winsome McDonald)

come to talk with
her himself.
Gather lots of
mints, mullein
stalk and sweet
(roots) lobelia
in garden.
sage tea—thyme
sassafras bark to
use—wild cherries
bark—Ginseng
used to be used a
good deal but she
never did [use] much
Willing to talk matters
over calm & composed
—thotful—very
considerate
not inclined to be
arbitr[ar]y.
Repartee—quick
cool in emergencies
never excited
Fred A cut arm
—with bottle—
blood running
she bathed it—
talked to him, got [him]
over his terror—used
camphor on things
like that.
[Grandmother] could say sharp
things—but usually
mild-spoken
Heard her speak
to tourist—who

(Sitting L-R) Vida Smith Smith, Alexander Hale Smith, Elizabeth Kendall Smith and Frederick Alexander Smith. (Standing L-R) Don Alvin Smith, Coral Smith Horner, Joseph George Smith, Emma Smith Kennedy and Arthur Marion Smith, Emma's son and family (Author's collection)

tried to probe into
her personal affairs
"Thank you—those
things are <u>personal</u>."
In-laws thot the
<u>world</u> of <u>her</u>—
Somebody tried to
quiz her abt why
she m[arried]. Maj.
Bidamon—her [reply was, "That is a]
private affair."—
Alex [Fred's father] said he believed
it was so the Western[66]
peop[le] would let her alone
[Major Bidamon] always treated her respectfully.
[Grandmother] showed no disapo
intment—didn't care
much of him, but
never revealed it—
made her boys
respect him.[67]
Once—he got drunk
on barrel of hard
cider—two or 3 days [later]
Alex said, "Mother
if you say so Ill
knock head [of]
barrell in & let
it out—"
She said, "No
let him alone.
if he didn't
drink that he'd
drink something
else—He goes to
bed & sleeps it

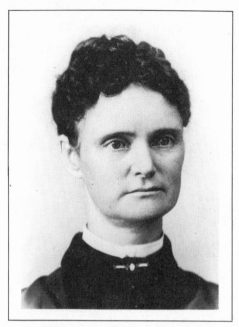

Elizabeth Kendall Smith, *Emma's daughter-in-law (Courtesy Gracia Denning)*

Alexander Hale Smith, *Emma's son (Courtesy Audio-Visual Department, Reorganized Church of Jesus Christ of Latter Day Saints)*

Elizabeth Kendall Smith, *Emma's daughter-in-law (Author's collection)*

Alexander Hale Smith, *Emma's son (Author's collection)*

off—let him alone."
[Grandmother] occasionally wore a
cap about house.
Hair always nicely
combed—
[Grandfather] Joseph considered her
advise good—sought it
& respected it. She
[was] loyal—sympathetic—
stood by all ways
[Grandfather Joseph Smith] often taken away
& she would wonder
if she'd ever see
him again.
Used grease to
get tar off
[his] skinned [and] bruised [body].[68]
Never found fault
—or complained
Alway[s] had a disposition
to make the best
of things. Hated
oppression—& would
fight for her rights
Able to get good out of
every condition
Incident. During big
polit[ical] camp[ai]gn several
candidates came to
[Mansion House] hotel for dinner
[Grandmother made] fritters. At the
meal served with honey or syrup.
delighted—[Politicians asked,] "What
do you call
these things?"
She said, "It all

Alexander Hale Smith, *Emma's son*
(Author's collection)

David Hyrum Smith, *Emma's son*
(Author's collection)

Joseph Smith, III, *Emma's son*
(Author's collection)

Alexander Hale Smith, *Emma's son*
(Author's collection)

depends
A year like this
we call them
<u>Candidates</u>"
all puffed up
& <u>air</u> in them.[69]
Affectionate in
her way but not
demonstrative—[Her] aff[ection]
was deep—but she
manifested it
quietly—in service
Raised a number
[of] children that were
not her own.[70]
Daughters in
law—[were] helped with
children [by Grandmother][71]—Excellent [care]
Joined Reorg[anization and was among] leading
members in Nauvoo[72]
—used to hold the
branch prayer meeting
in her big dining room
sing &c.—[Needed additional] chairs
Real meeting house upstairs
in [Grandfather Smith's] brick store—[73]
About one block West
of Mansion [House] Hotel
Mansion b[ui]lt 1842[74]
Nauvoo House near
River abt 1870[75]
[Grandmother] loved the River
[and] Nauvoo—
[She would] go with Alex[76]
or Joseph in boat
on river—cross

Lucy Mack Smith, *Emma's mother-in-law photograph of engraving (Author's collection)*

Hyrum Smith, *Emma's brother-in-law photograph of engraving (Author's collection)*

Samuel H.B. Smith, *Emma's nephew son of Samuel H. Smith (Courtesy LDS Church Archives)*

Ina Coolbrith, *Emma's niece daughter of Don Carlos Smith (Author's collection)*

river to [attend] meetings
in Montrose[77]
<u>Alex</u> very skillful[78]
[Grandfather Joseph Smith's] friends [were] ambitious—
to
make him Pres. U.S.
[He had] no particular ambition
[desired] justice.[79]
[Grandmother] Emma married in Nauvoo
[Mansion] House?[80]
[Resided in] Manchester [with] Joseph parents[81]
[Lived with] Isaac Hale [in Harmony, Pennsylvania][82]
[Lived with] Whitmer—[Fayette,] N.Y.[83]
[Lived with] Whitneys [Kirtland,] Ohio[84]
[Resided in] Far West [Missouri][85]
[Resided in] Quincy [Illinois][86]
Log [house at Commerce]—orig[inally] a fort
took up land—[87]
Nauvoo House
begun [in] 1842[88]
roof by Maj. B[idamon in]
1870 & [Grandmother] moved
in—up to 3rd
story—outer
wall stood for
years.[89]

———————

Grm[other] lived to see [the deaths
of many of her family][90]
1840 Joseph Sen[91]
1841 Don Carlos[92]
1844 Hy[ru]m & Joseph[93]
Samuel [H. Smith][94]
1855 [Lucy Mack Smith][95]

Frederick Granger Williams Smith, *Emma's son (Courtesy Audio-Visual Department,*
Reorganized Church of Jesus Christ of Latter Day Saints)

1862 Frederick died[96]
B Y[oung] took poss[ession of] record
of Ch[urc]h—private journal [of Grandfather Smith]
one man in Utah said
"If you folks ever
could have gotten
possession of that
Journal—you would
fixed & spoiled his
game"[97]
[John] Whitmer [and] B Y[oung]
took all private papers.[98]
[Grandmother was] broadminded,
liberal, not disposed
to take honor to herself.
a good deal like
my father (Joseph)[99]

S[iste]r <u>Short</u>[100]   54
            <u>11</u>
         1865[101]
Saw Grm[other]—Mansion
House—dark, tall lady
small sprigged lavender
calico dress—flour
sack pinned around
her—not hemmed
but clean.
David [Hyrum Smith][102] came in
[he was] tall slender youth
dressed ordinary
Some one took
her [Sister Short] over [to Mansion] house
remem[bers] people
more than house
[Sister Short saw] Grf[ather Smith's] military cap[103]

David Hyrum Smith, *Emma's son (Courtesy Audio-Visual Department, Reorganized Church of Jesus Christ of Latter Day Saints)*

Someone remarked
that Grf[ather] had said
he would to God
he'd never put
it on![104]
Maj. Bidamon said
(They wanted her [Grandmother] to
go to Cnf[erence] [at] String Prairie[105]
She thot she couldn't
go—& Major said
"O she thinks if
she leaves house the
bottom would drop
out of the well
while she was
gone."
David [Hyrum Smith] went to
Cnf[erence] & setting in
[open-air] meeting [in] (Arbor
with boughs) with
white h[an]dk[erchie]f sat
folding it into
rose petals—
beautiful white
<u>rose</u> out of his
hdkf—[106]
John Hawley[107]—[was] supp[osed]
to be good man.
when he died my fath[er, Alexander Hale Smith,]
said he was one
of the most
humble, honest
men he ever knew
His con[fidant and brother] Geo [Hawley][108] sent his biog
down to be printed
& it was pub[lished] without

(L-R) Frederick Alexander Smith, Israel Alexander Smith and Elbert Aoriul Smith, Emma's grandsons (Courtesy Audio-Visual Department, Reorganized Church of Jesus Christ of Latter Day Saints)

the references to polyg
Geo. was disati[sfied]
wanted mss
back. S[iste]r Short
read it very
intently ~~reading~~
He refered to
pressure being
brot to bear
on Grf[ather Smith] to produce
polyg.
Walter Smith[109] cut out
carets from mss. [110]
~~E C Brand~~[111]
T[homas] W Smith said[112]
to l[ea]v[e in Sister] Shorts parts[113]
that he [Thomas W. Smith] had visited
Emma ~~& she said~~ whom
he questioned
farther than
any one had &
she said certain
men read [in the] Bible
[about] polyg—had Joseph
Sr[114] ask Lord
to permit—Denied
Second time   "
Third time—if
you will—have it
so—<u>have it</u>
so. Hawley implied
[from this that] Hyrum [Smith] is
teach[in]g it—Expect[115]

Inez Smith Davis, *Emma's great-granddaughter*
(Author's collection)

Inez [Smith Davis][116]
said Mother[117] said Grm[other]
fond of lavender—later
years wore lavender almost
altogether
Taught [Audentia Anderson's] Aunt Lizzy to cook[118]
Wm. Marks [was] a friend[119]
Edmund Br[iggs][120]
Story about Grm[other's]
backache—plaster [was applied]
Elder offer[ed] prayer [for]
S[iste]r Emma
[to be] subservient to powers
that be—When
they got up [from prayer, she said,]—
"There's the door
You go out."
[Grandmother] appealed to Joseph
—He said "What
she says <u>goes</u>
here"—He <u>went</u>
She said "that
cured my backache."

*"**The Homestead**", Emma's first Nauvoo home, by her son,
David Hyrum Smith (Courtesy Lynn E. Smith)*

NOTES FOR
Frederick Alexander Smith's Reminiscences

*Frederick Alexander Smith (1862-1954) was Emma Hale Smith's first grandson. The eldest child of Alexander Hale Smith and Elizabeth Agnes Kendall, Frederick was born 19 January 1862 at Sonora, Hancock County, Illinois. He married Mary Angelina Walker and following her death he married Esther Clark. Frederick was active in the RLDS Church as a missionary, apostle and presiding patriarch. He died in June of 1954 at the age of ninety-two.

45. Arthur Marion Smith (1880-1964) was Emma Hale Smith's grandchild. The youngest son of Alexander Hale Smith and Elizabeth Agnes Kendall, he married Estella Danielson in 1904. In 1922, following the death of his first wife, Arthur married Minnie Smith. Originally a member of the RLDS Church, he later joined the Church of Christ Temple Lot where he was an active missionary until his death in 1964.

46. Joseph Smith, III.

47. See notes 30 and 32.

48. Elizabeth Revell, wife of Thomas Revell (RLDS branch president at Nauvoo), was present when Emma Hale Smith Bidamon died.

49. Emma Smith's selection of sacred hymns was first published in 1835 (actually the hymnal was not available until early 1836) and contained a preface and ninety untitled hymns. Only words were printed; no music was included. Forty-two of the hymns had appeared earlier in Church periodicals. At least thirty-four had been authored by Mormons. The second edition of the hymnal was published in 1841 in Nauvoo. This edition was much larger; it included three hundred and four titled hymns and a tempo was indicated for each. The little hymnal was very much in demand and plans were under way for a third edition in early 1843. While there is no evidence that this contemplated third edition was ever printed, Emma did select hymns for the first RLDS hymnal which was published in 1861 and enlarged in 1864.

50. See photograph of watercolor on page 143. In 1974 two ivory-handled riding crops of Emma Hale Smith were in the possession of James Brandon Horner, Emma's great-grandson, Ronan, Montana.

51. The striking out of this word undoubtedly attests to the fact that Emma Smith never wore earrings.

52. Emma Smith's ring, a cornelian stone or moss agate, is now in the possession of Mrs. Lorene Smith, Independence, Missouri.

53. Excited by liquor and hatred, a mob with blackened faces dragged Joseph Smith from his bed during the night of 24 March 1832. Choking him into submission, they stripped him naked, scratched his skin with their fingernails, poured hot tar in his open wounds, tore hair from his head and then daubed his body with feathers. In the mob's attempt to force Joseph to drink a vial of poison, his front tooth was broken. Emma, with members of the Johnson family, spent the night removing the tar from Joseph's body.

54. Reference is made to the horrid deaths of Joseph and Hyrum Smith in Carthage Jail on 27 June 1844.

55. The bodies of the Church's Prophet and Patriarch lay in state on 29 June 1844 at the Mansion House while thousands filed silently past the coffins to pay their last respects. William W. Phelps preached their funeral sermon in the grove.

56. Following the Saints' viewing of the bodies of the martyrs on 29 June 1844, the coffins were properly weighted and in a public session were conveyed to a Nauvoo Temple burial vault. However, the bodies were secretly interred in the basement of the unfinished Nauvoo House. Approximately six months later, they were secretly disinterred and reburied adjacent to the family cemetery on the Old Homestead property; Emma and Joseph's first Nauvoo residence.

57. Emma Smith's remains were interred in a brick vault, south of the Old Homestead, along side the concealed grave of her husband. In 1928 the inscribed stone slab that served as a lid to the burial vault was cut into three pieces and used as separate markers for the graves of Emma, Joseph and Hyrum Smith—their skeletal remains were dug up and reinterred at this time. In December 1867 Emma Smith wrote to her son: "I would like to know something about that graveyard fence . . .and what you think about trying to have it put up the coming spring. I have always felt sad about the

neglected condition of that place, and as I do not expect to be able to build me a house to live in, I would like to fix a place to be put away in when I have done all my work on the earth" (Emma Smith to Joseph Smith, III, 2 December 1867, RLDS Library-Archives).

Samuel O. Bennion was present when the skeletal remains of Emma, Joseph and Hyrum Smith were unearthed in mid-January 1928 and reported that "Emma Smith's body was also taken up and placed right by Joseph's in the same kind of a concrete form. Her body was not as well preserved as the Martyrs were....I am fully convinced that these skeletons were the bones of [Emma,] Joseph and Hyrum and since they were taken from their resting place I am very thankful I was there" (Samuel O. Bennion to Heber J. Grant and Counselors, 21 January 1928, Church Archives).

58. The text refers to landscape markings used to identify the concealed graves of the martyrs. The graves were situated adjacent to or beneath the small brick house (10 × 12) directly north of Emma's grave.

59. "She cooked coffee in a big pot in the kitchen but it was served from a huge pewter urn, with a fanciful lid, spigot, and spout. It later became a cookie jar....She had also a cookie jar like a small churn which was *never empty* and the children could go to it whenever they were hungry day or night. Her cookies were usually a little sweeter and richer than biscuit[s] but not so rich as regular cookies or doughnuts....Emma's doughnuts were always the twisted kind" (Vesta Crawford Notes).

60. Frederick Alexander Smith moved from Nauvoo with his father's family to Harrison County, Missouri, in 1876.

61. Of her belief in the Book of Mormon Emma Smith said in 1879: "My belief is that the Book of Mormon is of divine authenticity—I have not the slightest doubt of it. I am satisfied that no man could have dictated the writing of the manuscripts unless he was inspired" (*The History of the Reorganized Church of Jesus Christ of Latter Day Saints, 1844-1872* [Independence: Herald Publishing House, 1896], 3:357). In Nauvoo in May 1863 Emma testified that "she had allwise beleaved the B of M, and the Doc & Covenants from their first being published and had never doubted them but she knew they were true" (Diary of Edmund C. Briggs, 24 May 1863, RLDS Library-Archives).

62. Evidence attests that the Prophet Joseph Smith desired that his son should succeed him as president of the Church at his death and so

blessed Joseph, III, on 17 January 1844. Yet the realization of this blessing was predicated upon certain conditions, and as Brigham Young and the Twelve Apostles understood it, this included acceptance of and adherence to the full gospel program that the Prophet had established prior to his death (i.e., sealing keys of the priesthood). (Concerning his designation as his father's successor, see deposition of Joseph Smith, III, in "Temple Lot Case," Eighth Circuit Court, 1892.)

63. Emma felt a need to leave Nauvoo after the Mormon exodus to the Great Basin because there had been threats that all members of the Smith family would be killed. Emma left with her children for Fulton City, Whiteside County, Illinois, on 12 September 1846, two days after the commencement of the "Battle of Nauvoo." They traveled on the steamer, *Uncle Toby*, and Emma rented a house just on the edge of town. When Emma learned that the renters of the Mansion House were planning to vacate it and take some of the family furniture, she and her family returned posthaste to Nauvoo by land, arriving 19 February 1847. Fulton City was a natural place to go for safety because family friend, William Marks, had removed to that city, and members of Emma's immediate family (the Hales) were residing in nearby Lee County, Illinois.

64. Emma detailed to her son, Joseph, the procedure for making her medicinal salve:

> Of sweet elder bark, a good large handful after it is scraped and as much gymson leaves and buds if they are green and tender enough to be p[o]unded up fine, put them in a skillet or small kettle, and cover them with water, and boil them about twenty minutes. Then take it off and when cool enough strain the liquor through a cloth that is strong enough, wringing so as to get out all the dregs that can be got. Then put the liquor back into the kettle and boil it about half away. Then put a half pound of mutton tallow, half a pound of beeswax [in], and let it simmer down to a fry, then take it off and put one ounce of camphor gum into it, and stir it, keeping it warm till the gum is all dissolved. Try it on a rag, and if too soft, put a little more beeswax in, and if too hard a little tallow. If you want a salve that will draw take a part of what is made and dissolve a small piece of rosin in it. Now if you didn't save any gymson last fall, you can make it with elder alone. The first camphorated salve I ever made was just mutton tallow and beeswax and camphor alone and it was then thought to be an excellent article. (Emma Bidamon to Joseph Smith, III, 20 January 1867, RLDS Library-Archives.)

65. Brooks R. Hamilton, a native of Pennsylvania, is the physician referred to in the text.

66. "Western" referred to Mormons in Utah.

67. Romantic aspects of Emma's marriage to "Major" Bidamon most likely began to wane after he fathered an illegitimate child in 1864.

68. Joseph Smith was tarred and feathered in Hiram, Ohio, on 24 March 1832. Lard was obtained from Elsa Johnson which was rubbed on the Prophet's body to remove the tar.

69. "Once in [the Prophet] Joseph's time, when a number of candidates & politicians came to her house for dinner & not having been notified of their coming, [Emma] made a hasty dessert of a sort of fritter fried in fat. They were a hollow ball of pastry served with sauce or cream & sugar. One of the guests complimented her & asked what she called them. She smiled & answered soberly that they were called 'candidates' " (Vesta Crawford Notes).

70. These children would have included Charles Edward Bidamon and Elizabeth Agnes Kendall.

71. Emma would have assisted the following daughters-in-law: Emmeline Griswold Smith (wife of Joseph Smith, III), Bertha Madison Smith (second wife of Joseph Smith, III); Annie Maria Jones (wife of Frederick Granger Williams Smith); Elizabeth Agnes Kendall (wife of Alexander Hale Smith); and Clara Charlotte Hartshorn (wife of David Hyrum Smith).

72. The RLDS congregation at Nauvoo was known as the "Olive Branch."

73. Members of the RLDS branch at Nauvoo met in the "Red Brick Store," also known as the Prophet's store. The store had been opened for business on 5 January 1842. In the upper level of the building was a large meeting room called the "Lodge Room" or "General Business Office." This chamber accommodated a variety of meeting functions. The store was located on Water Street, block 155, about one block west of the Mansion House.

74. The Mansion House was not completed until the fall of 1843. See note 15.

75. See note 14.

76. Alexander Hale Smith, son of Emma Hale and Joseph Smith, Jr., was born 2 June 1838, at Far West, Missouri. Emma's third son to survive birth, Alexander strongly resembled his father physically, his penetrating blue eyes and the absence of wrinkles on the forehead. He married Elizabeth Agnes Kendall on 23 June 1861 and they were the parents of nine children. A fearless missionary for the RLDS Church, he also served as an apostle and first patriarch of that church. He died at the Mansion House in Nauvoo, Illinois, 11 August 1909.

77. Montrose, Lee County, Iowa.

78. Alexander Hale Smith was a very skillful hunter of wild game.

79. On 29 January 1844 Joseph Smith and a few close friends decided to press for his candidacy to the United States presidency. The National Reform party confirmed his nomination in a state convention at Nauvoo on 17 May 1844. According to Emma Smith (as reported by W.W. Blair), the Prophet's close associates urged him to seek nomination for the presidency: "During the evening [8 April 1860] Sister Emma related many incidents in respect to church affairs which were both interesting and instructive. She said Joseph, her former husband, very reluctantly consented to allow his name placed in nomination for the Presidency of the United States, a matter urged upon him by two or more consecutive councils in Nauvoo, prominent in which were Brigham Young and some others of the Twelve. She stated that in those times his attention was so taken up with persistent appeals from ambitious, aspiring men, that good men like Father [William] Marks did not have much chance to be heard by him. Joseph at first pronounced the scheme unwise and uncalled for. In this Sister Emma concurred, but their judgment was overruled and Joseph yielded on the claim set forth by his blind political advisers, that in permitting his name to go prominently before the Nation and the world in a political way, it would give popularity and impetus to the work of the church" (*Memoirs of W.W. Blair*, comp. Frederick B. Blair [Lamoni, Iowa: Herald Publishing, 1908], p. 32).

80. Sarah M. Kimball, writing from Nauvoo to Marinda Nancy Hyde

in 1848, gave the details of Emma's wedding: "The marriage of Mrs Smith is the all absorbing topic of conversation. She was married last thursday eve the groom Mr Bidimen is I believe looked upon with universal contempt he was a widower wears a wig [and] married Emmy [Emma] for her property....The bride was dressed in plum colored sattin a lace tuck hankerchief gold watch & chain no cap hair plain....The eve brought a grand shiveree & the following night a ball was given" (Sarah M. Kimball to Marinda Hyde, 2 January 1848, Church Archives).

81. Emma and Joseph Smith lived with his parents in Manchester, New York, January-December 1827.

82. Emma and Joseph Smith moved to Harmony, Pennsylvania, in December 1827 and it was their permanent residence until August 1830.

83. Emma and Joseph Smith lived with the Peter Whitmer, Sr., family in Fayette, New York, during the final days of translation of the Book of Mormon in 1829, and also resided with them for a time in the fall of 1830.

84. Emma and Joseph Smith lived with the Newel K. Whitney family in Kirtland, Ohio, on a temporary basis in early 1831, and in September 1832 they moved into the upper story of Whitney's Kirtland store. Here they remained for a few years.

85. Emma and Joseph Smith moved from Kirtland, Ohio, to Far West, Missouri, during January of 1838, arriving 14 March 1838. Emma and children remained in Missouri until February 1839.

86. During Joseph Smith's Missouri incarcerations, Emma and children left Missouri and settled temporarily near Quincy, Illinois, with John and Sarah Cleveland.

87. After the Prophet's escape from Missouri law-enforcement officers in April 1839, he rejoined Emma and their children. They moved to Commerce (later Nauvoo) and took up residence in the Old Homestead (May 1839).

88. The cornerstone of the Nauvoo House was laid by Joseph Smith on 2 October 1841. Although never completed, the Nauvoo House was intended to accommodate distinguished visitors in a facility "unrivaled in the western country." It was hoped that the Nauvoo House (and temple) would attract men of wealth, character and influence to come to Nauvoo

and there be converted to Mormonism. See note 14. When construction of the Nauvoo House lagged, Joseph decided to add a wing for boarders onto his new Mansion House (then being built) which in some measure satisfied the need for a comfortable waterfront hotel. John C. Calhoun, Jr., visited the Mormon city in June 1844, agreed that Nauvoo was "the most beautiful [site] in the Western World" and described his meeting the Mormon leader: "From Quincy we Started for Nauvoo, and arrived there after dark, it was the evening after the Governor had Sent to arest Joe Smith, and the City in consequence in a great State of excitement, a large number of us being anxious to See the Prophet, begged the Captain of the boat to wait two or three hours for us, and in a few minutes after, found ourselves in an Omnibus, rolling rapidly through water Street, and Soon our horses were drawn up before the door of the hotel, kept by the Prophet himself.... Upon telling him the purpose of our visit, he invited us to the drawing-room, where he soon joined us, he gave us a full description of his difficulties, and also an exposition of his faith, frequently calling himself the Prophet, in the course of conversation" (John C. Calhoun, Jr., to "My dear brother", 19 July 1844, Special Collections, University of South Carolina Library).

89. See photograph on page 58.

90. Emma's father, Isaac Hale, died 11 January 1839 at Harmony, Pennsylvania. Her mother, Elizabeth Lewis Hale, died 16 February 1842, at Harmony, Pennsylvania. Her brother, Jesse Hale, died 2 December 1874. Her brother, David Hale, died 16 April 1878. Her brother, Alva Hale, died about 1862. Her sister, Phebe Hale, died 25 December 1856 or 57. Her sister, Tryal Hale Morse, was killed 3 June 1860. Emma's first child, Alvin Smith, lived one day and died 16 June 1828. Her twins, Thadeus and Louisa Smith, lived one day and died 1 May 1831. Joseph Murdock Smith, Emma's adopted son, died in late March 1832. Her son, Don Carlos Smith, died 15 August 1841. And finally she was delivered of an unnamed stillborn son on 6 February 1842.

91. Emma's father-in-law, Joseph Smith, Sr., died 14 September 1840 at Nauvoo.

92. Emma's brother-in-law, Don Carlos Smith, died 8 August 1841 at Nauvoo.

93. Hyrum and Joseph Smith were murdered on 27 June 1844.

94. Samuel Harrison Smith, Emma's brother-in-law, died 30 July 1844 across the street from the Mansion House.

95. Emma's mother-in-law, Lucy Mack Smith, died 14 May 1856 (*not* in 1855 as erroneously published in numerous sources), in the Mansion House.

96. Frederick Granger Williams Smith was the second surviving son of Emma Hale and Joseph Smith. Born 20 June 1836 in Kirtland, Ohio, he married Annie Maria Jones 13 September 1857, and they were the parents of one child: Alice Fredericka Smith. Frederick died 13 April 1862 from injuries received by a kick from a horse. His daughter, Alice Fredericka, was born 27 November 1858, in Nauvoo, Illinois, and was the first of Emma's descendants to join the Utah Church (6 January 1915). Even so, she subsequently was baptized a member of the RLDS Church and died unmarried 5 February 1932.

97. Joseph Smith's letterbooks, private diaries and other Church minute books were in the possession of Willard Richards and William Clayton at the time the Prophet was killed and were subsequently taken to Utah.

98. John Whitmer, ordained Church Historian in April 1831, retained possession of his history of the Church (1831-38) when he was excommunicated in March 1838. See also note 97.

99. Frederick Alexander Smith's father, Alexander Hale Smith, very much resembled the Prophet Joseph Smith in stature and facial feature.

100. Viola I. Vernon Short, wife of Morris T. Short, was the author of *The Fourth Relaford* (1928). She and her sister-in-law, Eva Bailey Short, were founders of the Pen and Ink Club of the RLDS Church.

101. Born 28 April 1854, Viola V. Short was eleven years old when she visited with Emma in Nauvoo.

102. See note 30.

103. The text refers to the Prophet Joseph Smith's Nauvoo Legion bicorn hat. See photograph on page 142.

104. There is a Smith family tradition that the Prophet's high office in

the Nauvoo militia and his involvement in local, state and national politics were directly responsible for his death at Carthage.

105. A branch of the RLDS Church was located at String Prairie, Iowa.

106. David Hyrum Smith constantly occupied himself artistically.

107. John Hawley was born in Hancock County, Illinois, 4 March 1826. Converted to the Mormon Church in the 1830s, he associated with Lyman Wight's colony in Texas after the martyrdom, later supported the leadership of the Twelve Apostles, and finally joined the Reorganization in 1868. He married Sylvia Johnson on 22 October 1848 and they were the parents of twelve children. Hawley died at Lamoni, Iowa, of pneumonia on 17 April 1909.

108. John Hawley's autobiography, written in January 1885, is located at the RLDS Library-Archives.

109. Walter Smith was editor of the RLDS *Journal of History* and succeeded Heman C. Smith as RLDS Church Historian in June 1919.

110. Only a small part of John Hawley's autobiography was published. The handwritten manuscript bears editorial markings on many pages.

111. E.C. Brand, born in England 22 February 1822, was a Mormon convert that joined the RLDS Church in December 1863 in San Francisco, California. He served as a senior president of the First Quorum of Seventy in the RLDS Church and died 12 October 1890 in Kansas.

112. Thomas Wood Smith, born 7 March 1838 in Philadelphia, Pennsylvania, was converted to the RLDS Church by Jason Briggs in 1866. He was called to the RLDS apostleship in 1873 and died 27 May 1894 in Independence, Missouri.

113. Sister Viola Short, a writer and editor, apparently made alterations to John Hawley's manuscript for publication. See text at note 110.

114. The text is referring to the Prophet Joseph Smith.

115. Surprisingly, Hyrum Smith's knowledge of his brother's teaching and practice of plural marriage in Nauvoo lagged far behind inauguration of the practice in 1841. Hyrum first manifested strong opposition to the doctrine and practice when he learned of it in the spring of 1843, but was converted on 26 May 1843, with the help of Brigham Young.

116. Vida Inez Smith Davis, Emma Hale Smith's great-grandchild, was the daughter of Vida Elizabeth Smith (Alexander Hale Smith's daughter) and Heman Conoman Smith. Born 16 January 1889 at Lamoni, Iowa, she assisted her father in the RLDS historian's office and later authored a one-volume history of the RLDS Church. She married James William Davis on 12 June 1913, and had no children. She died 24 October 1964 in Independence, Missouri.

117. The text is referring to Elizabeth Kendall Smith, Frederick Alexander Smith's mother.

118. "Aunt Lizzy" refers to Audentia Anderson's aunt, Elizabeth Kendall Smith.

119. William Marks, born 15 November 1792 in Rutland, Vermont, was converted to the Mormon Church about 1835 and served as a stake president in Kirtland, Ohio, and Nauvoo, Illinois. Although Marks was a close friend to Joseph Smith, his unwillingness to support fully the practice of plural marriage left him somewhat estranged from the Prophet and members of the Twelve Apostles at the martyrdom in June 1844. With some ambivalence he rejected the right of the Twelve Apostles to lead the Church after the Prophet's death and finally rallied behind the Reorganization where he served as a counselor in the First Presidency until his death in Plano, Illinois, 22 May 1872.

120. One of fifteen children, Edmund Briggs was born 20 February 1835 in Wheeler, Steuben County, New York. He was the "pioneer" missionary for the RLDS Church, and later served as a member of its quorum of Twelve Apostles. He died 4 July 1913 in Independence, Missouri.

Elbert Aoriul Smith, *Emma's grandson*
(Author's collection)

Elbert Aoriul Smith
Reminiscences*

Elbert
Milk—broken steps
strained milk up
stairs, & dropped
she wouldn't go
up stairs any more[121]
Blackberries
father [David Hyrum Smith] ate in pantry
[and got] ill—[Grandmother Smith] did not
rebuke [him]. At next
meal time [she put a] dish
bef[ore]. him [and] urged him
to eat—more &
more—much rather
She had whipped him.
Inn [Mansion House]—light biscuits
—candidates—
Political com[mi]t[tee]
Why? Because
so full of wind.[122]
Mormon elder
visited [Grandmother] plead [with] her
to go to Utah—
Red-headed—
angry—proposed
marriage. "She
would yet kneel

Emma Smith Bidamon, circa 1875 (Courtesy Audio-Visual Department, Reorganized
Church of Jesus Christ of Latter Day Saints)

down to me" [he said]
[She said] "If I do it will
be the first
red headed
Brighamite I
ever bowed down
to."[123]
[At] Fulton City—[Grandmother Smith explained,] "I
made up my mind
I had no friend
left but God &
no place to go
but home."[124]
—Amboy—tempestuous
crossing 1860[125]—whenever
she had work to
do the Old Boy
tri[e]d to defeat it. [126]

Clara Hartshorn Smith,
Emma's daughter-in-law
(Author's collection)

Elbert Aoriul Smith, *Emma's grand-*
son (Author's collection)

David Hyrum Smith,
Emma's son
(Courtesy Lynn E. Smith)

NOTES FOR
Elbert Aoriul Smith Reminiscences

*Elbert Aoriul Smith, Emma Hale Smith's grandson, was the only child of David Hyrum Smith and Clara Charlotte Hartshorn. Born 8 March 1871 at the Mansion House in Nauvoo, Elbert served as a member of the RLDS First Presidency from 1909 to 1938, and as Presiding Patriarch from 1938 to 1958. He married Clara Cochran 4 September 1895 at Lamoni, Iowa, and they were the parents of three children. Elbert died 15 May 1959 at Independence, Missouri.

121. "The barn was in the rear to one side of the Mansion House, the lower story was of stone and the upper of brick. The milk was kept in the basement story of the [Mansion] house. She had asked her second husband Bidamon many times to repair the stairs to this basement or cellar and he did not do it. Then she delivered an ultimatum that she would not again carry milk down the stairs until they were fixed. So she threw the pan of milk down the stairs that night and quietly proceeded with her kitchen duties. Bidamon mended the stairs forthwith" (Vesta Crawford Notes).

122. See note 69.

123. It has traditionally been believed that the "red-headed Brig-hamite" who proposed marriage to Emma was Almon W. Babbitt. It was common knowledge that there was no love lost between sandy-haired Brigham Young and Emma Smith. The reality of their personality conflict is also reflected in the above statement by Emma.

124. A variation of this statement is found in E. Cecil McGavin, *Nauvoo the Beautiful* (Salt Lake City: Stevens and Wallis, Inc., 1946), p. 191.

125. On the morning of 4 April 1860, Emma and her son, Joseph Smith, III, crossed the Mississippi in a small skiff, then proceeded to the Burlington, Iowa, train depot. They were assisted in this rough passage by family friend, James Gifford, who braved the rain and cold with them. Emma was accompanying her son to the RLDS Church conference at Amboy, Illinois, where on 6 April, Joseph Smith, III, was accepted as prophet, seer, revelator and successor to his father by that body.

126. The "Old Boy" is a reference to Satan.

Alice Fredericka Smith, *Emma's granddaughter*
(Courtesy H.G. "Bud" Fredrick, Jr.)

Don Alvin Smith *and **Eva Grace Smith***
Emma's grandchildren (Author's Collection)

David Carlos Smith *and **Mary Audentia***
Smith*, Emma's grandchildren*
(Author's Collection)

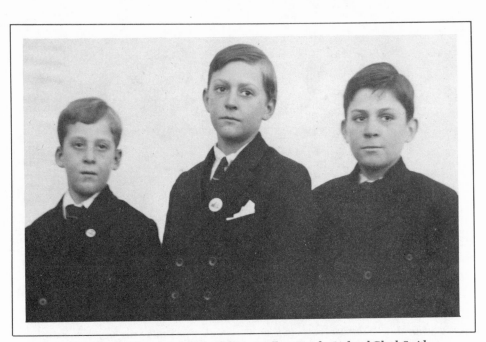

(L-R) **Reginald Archer Smith, William Wallace Smith, Richard Clark Smith,**
Emma's Grandchildren (Author's Collection)

Bertha Madison Smith, *Emma's daughter-in-law (Author's collection)*

Ada Clark Smith, *Emma's daughter-in-law (Courtesy Alma R. Blair)*

Lucy Smith Millikin, *Emma's sister-in-law (Courtesy LDS Church Archives)*

Katherine Smith Salisbury, *Emma's sister-in-law (Author's collection)*

Frederick Madison Smith, *Emma's grandson*
(Author's collection)

Israel Alexander Smith, *Emma's grandson*
(Author's collection)

William Smith, *Emma's brother-in-law*
(Courtesy RLDS Archives)

William Wallace Smith, *Emma's grandson*
(Author's collection)

The Mansion House, 1904 Emma's second Nauvoo residence (Courtesy Brigham Young University Library Archives)

"The Homestead" and Emma's grave, 1904 (Courtesy Brigham Young University Library Archives).

Smith Family/6 November 1912
(Sitting, children L-R) Joseph Arthur McCallum, Homer Alexander McCallum, Carol Rogene Smith, Lois Audentia Smith, Lucy Rogene Anderson, Smith DeWalt Lysinger, Philip Eugene Lysinger. **(Sitting on steps)** Glenna Marie Kennedy, Corlie Corrine McCallum, Robert Montfort McCallum. **(Sitting adults)** Carrie Lucinda (Smith) Weld, Emma Josepha (Smith) McCallum, Joseph Smith III, Ada Rachel (Clark) Smith. **(Standing on ground)** Reginald Archer Smith, Israel Alexander Smith, Mary Audentia (Smith) Anderson, Hale Washington Smith, Lucy Yeteve (Smith) Lysinger, Frederick Madison Smith, Richard Clark Smith, Duane Smith Anderson. **(Standing on steps)** Richard Savery Salyards, Alice Myrmida Smith, Benjamin M. Anderson. **(Standing on porch)** Corlie (Montfort) McCallum, Bertha Aldine Smith (Baby), Rogene (Munsell) Smith, Emma Rebecca Weld, Doris Zuleika Anderson, Bertha Audentia Anderson, Ruth (Cobb) Smith, Roger Alexander Kennedy, Emma Belle (Smith) Kennedy.

Smith Family/Late 1915

1st Row (Seated L-R) Louis Brainerd Horner, Smith DeWalt Lysinger, Philip Eugene Lysinger, Lynn Elbert Smith, Elizabeth Grace Horner, Marion Don Smith, Maxwell Alexis Smith.

2nd Row: Robert George Badham (Baby), Walter George Badham, Heman Conoman Smith, Vida Elizabeth (Smith) Smith, Clara Charlotte (Hartshorn) Smith, Elizabeth Agnes (Kendall) Smith, Ina Lorena Horner (Baby), Ina Inez (Smith) Wright, Lois Audentia Smith, Coral Cecile Rebecca (Smith) Horner, James Brandon Horner (Child), Doris Rae Lysinger, Susan Zenetta (Pearsall) Smith, LaJune Harriett Smith

3rd Row: Joy May Smith, Winsome Lavinia Smith, Freda Saloam Smith, Harold LeGrande Smith, Lucy Yeteve (Smith) Lysinger, Clara Abigail (Cochran) Smith, Ronald Gibson Smith, Mary Angelina (Walker) Smith, Frederick Alexander Smith, Frederick Madison Smith, Ruth Lyman (Cobb) Smith, Alice Myrmida Smith, Emma Rebecca Weld, Beatrice Adelle Smith.

4th Row: Velora Belle Smith, Carrie Lucinda (Smith) Weld, Zadie Aileen Salyards, Richard Savery Salyards, Elbert Aoriul Smith, Jesse Melvin Lysinger, Avis (Hopkins) Smith, Glaud Leslie Smith, Francis Marion Weld, Frederick Augenstein Smith.

Joseph Smith, Jr., Nauvoo Legion uniform, watercolor by Sutcliffe Maudsley, 1842
(Author's collection)

Emma Hale Smith, riding habit, watercolor by Sutcliffe Maudsley, 1842
(Author's collection)

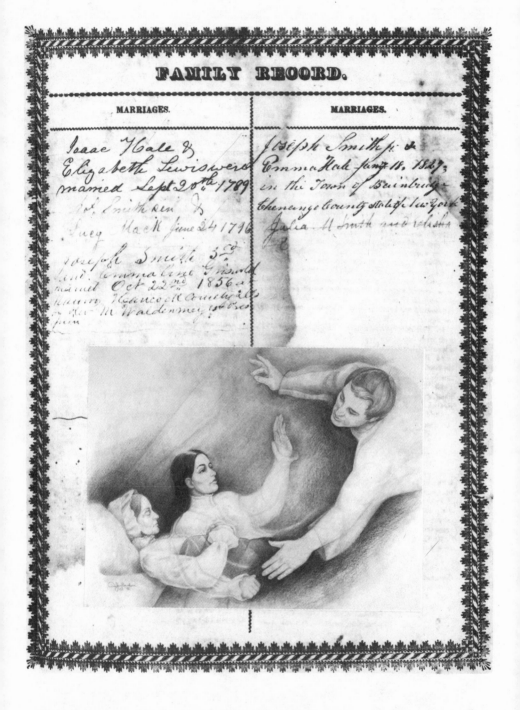

Marriage entry page from family Bible of Joseph Smith, Jr., and Emma Hale Smith (Author's collection) and "Emma's Deathbed Vision," by Dee Jay Bawden, March 1982

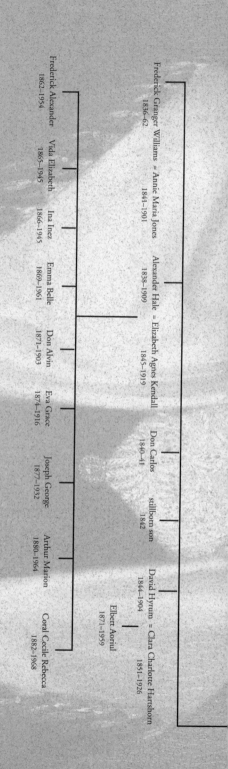

Frederick Granger Williams = Annie Maria Jones
1836–62   1841–1901

Alexander Hale = Elizabeth Agnes Kendall
1838–1909   1845–1919

Don Carlos
1840–41

stillborn son
1842

David Hyrum = Clara Charlotte Harshorn
1844–1904   1851–1926

Frederick Alexander
1862–1954

Vida Elizabeth
1865–1945

Ina Inez
1866–1945

Emma Belle
1869–1961

Don Alvin
1871–1903

Eva Grace
1874–1916

Joseph George
1877–1932

Arthur Marion
1880–1964

Coral Cecil Rebecca
1882–1968

Elbert Aoriul
1871–1959